T0076797

LEADERSHIP
OFFENSE

HarperCollins
Leadership

An Imprint of HarperCollins

LEADERSHIP
OFFENSE

MASTERING APPRAISAL, PERFORMANCE,
AND PROFESSIONAL DEVELOPMENT

PAUL FALCONE

Published by HarperCollins Leadership, an imprint of HarperCollins Focus LLC.

Published in association with Kevin Anderson & Associates: https://www.ka-writing.com/.

Topic 1: From "The Leader-as-Coach: 10 Questions You Need to Ask to Develop Employees." *SHRM HR Daily Newsletter*, October 24, 2016. Copyright 2016 by the Society for Human Resource Management. **Topic 18:** From "5 Strategies to Motivate Burned Out Workers." *SHRM HR Daily Newsletter*, July 12, 2019. Copyright 2019 by the Society for Human Resource Management. **Topic 15:** From "Amending Your Performance Review Template for the COVID-19 Pandemic." *SHRM HR Daily Newsletter*, September 11, 2020. Copyright 2020 by the Society for Human Resource Management. **Topic 19:** From "Servant Leadership for a New Generation." *SHRM HR Daily Newsletter*, July 17, 2021. Copyright 2021 by the Society for Human Resource Management. **Topic 20:** From "How to Be a 'Favorite Boss.'" *SHRM HR Daily Newsletter*, May 22, 2020. Copyright 2020 by the Society for Human Resource Management. All of the above used by permission of the publisher. All rights reserved.

ISBN 978-1-4002-3011-2 (eBook)
ISBN 978-1-4002-3004-4 (TP)

Library of Congress Control Number: 2021951253

Printed in the United States of America
22 23 24 25 26 LSC 10 9 8 7 6 5 4 3 2 1

CONTENTS

PART 3

INTRODUCTION

Leadership offense, like leadership defense, draws on common terms from the sports world to get us all on the same page. After all, most of us know the difference between any team's offensive and defensive roles and strategies, whether you're talking football, basketball, baseball, hockey, or just about any other sport. Interestingly enough, this same paradigm applies to the business world and, more specifically, to leadership. After all, building the muscle of your organization's frontline leadership team is the whole goal of the *Paul Falcone Workplace Leadership Series*, and in building that muscle for your entire team, you're likewise building it for yourself. Once leadership muscles are honed and developed, you can continue to nurture them—and rely on them—for the rest of your career. Do it right and get it right up front by establishing strong habits, and then benefit from this dedicated exercise forever more. That's a wise investment with a great return.

The offensive side of leadership is just what you're thinking: How do you motivate and retain staff? How do you create a work environment where people feel engaged and look to expend discretionary effort, both for their immediate manager's sake as well as for the company's? What does it take to get someone to fall in love with their organization and reach their own personal best at work? Even more significantly, how do you channel the energy and efforts of your highest performers to "move the middle"—those employees who make up 70 percent of the organization and who may be performing well in general but lack the passion and personal commitment to do their best work every day?

Sounds like such huge questions that you could write a book about it, right? That's because these elements of human and organizational behavior are the primary profit levers of your enterprise. Think about it: proprietary products last only for so long before patents run out, technical and software competitive advantages are fleeting and eventually get consumed by the broader market, and time-bound advantages (for example, low interest rates) will expire at some point, leaving you to rely on something else to set your organization apart from its competition. So, what helps one company distinguish itself from others over the long haul? The human capital asset. The human beings who create, sell, and distribute the product in manufacturing, sales, marketing, and distribution; the internal support teams that care for those asset-generating departments, like human resources, IT, and finance; and the senior leadership team that ensures that sufficient revenue and profits are generated to keep the organization healthy.

Without a doubt, no true leadership development program can get far without a keen focus on the motivations, engagement, commitment, accountability, and other positive considerations that make people happy at work and that create a healthy environment. So how do you create that state on a consistent and sustainable basis? Book 3 represents our opportunity to explore positivity at work, the importance of recognition, the value of the learning curve, and the critical nature of selfless leadership, open communication, and successful teambuilding.

Let's prepare to explore what it means to coach (rather than "manage") employees. Let's look at creating a performance management system that encourages high productivity and holds everyone accountable to delivering at the highest levels. And let's pull back the curtain on what it takes to build a leadership development program that not only attracts the best and brightest but retains them while they garner achievements and build new skills over time. This is definitely within your reach, both as an individual contributor and as a leader. You can create this level of awareness for those you are entrusted to lead and mentor. You can likewise pay this forward by passing your philosophy, teaching, and professional development strategies along to those who report to you and ultimately follow in your footsteps.

Leadership is the greatest gift the workplace offers because it gives you the opportunity to positively influence others' lives and create more leaders in turn. Let's work together to build this muscle, hone this craft, and create this philosophy that helps us excel, immediately benefits those whom we lead, and provides a competitive advantage to your organization. You are the talent asset; you are the profit lever. Now is the opportunity to reinvent, reflect, facilitate, include, and amplify others assigned to your care. It's time to make your world bigger, to expand your line of sight, and to recognize and appreciate the awesome opportunity you hold as a leader. I consider myself so fortunate to engage and accompany you in this adventure!

DISCLAIMER

Note: Throughout this book, I interchange the use of *his* and *her*, and I provide examples of fictitious men and women.

Obviously, all situations described in these pages can apply to anyone. Further, please bear in mind at all times that this book is not intended as a legal guide to the complex issues surrounding your employment practices. Because the book does not purport to render legal advice, it should not be used in place of a licensed practicing attorney when proper legal counsel and guidance become necessary. You must rely on your attorney to render a legal opinion that is related to actual fact situations.

CREATING A
COACHING CULTURE

Leadership success is directly measured by the success of those working on your team: their success is your success. It follows that the skills that made you successful as an individual contributor won't necessarily apply to your role as leader. As a leader, you should strive to create a "coaching culture" that focuses on selflessness and otherness; a concern that those who report to you grow, both personally and professionally; a dedication to listening with empathy and helping people find their way through their challenges rather than just giving them answers; and a personal commitment to those who have been entrusted to your care via your managerial leadership role in your organization.

You might stop right here and think, "Wait. I'm not here to be a career adviser to my people. There's work to be done, and they'll need to figure out how to be successful, just as I had to figure it out. No hand-holding and coddling on my team—I hate to say it's sink or swim, but, hey, if it worked for me, it should work for them."

Let's have another look at your premise, though. Although there's no right or wrong answer, it's possible that your initial reaction is a bit out of touch with the times. First, understand that Millennials and Gen Z currently make up 50 percent of the workforce as of this writing, and that percentage will increase dramatically as the last of the Baby Boomers near retirement around 2030. What do these younger generations want? Career mentoring and professional development, corporate social responsibility, commitment to environmental activism, and a more diverse and inclusive workforce. Do those ideals sound too lofty to you to be real? They're not. They're actually healthy and well thought out, meaning that if you don't meet at least some of these needs from a corporate strategy standpoint, you may be left lacking (that is, suffering from premature turnover or lackluster organizational performance).

Further, a quick look at the future of our workforce points to the following key trends:

- As robotics, artificial intelligence, and the gig economy grow, jobs are being reinvented, and people's expectations surrounding work, roles, and career paths are changing along with them.
- Fundamental skills such as critical thinking, problem-solving, communication, and emotional intelligence are the building blocks upon which our future economy will rely.
- Employer needs will focus more and more on leadership and social influence, innovation, complex problem-solving, and learning and active listening abilities.

In short, the new economy will require knowledge workers who often know more about their work than their boss does. They'll be easier to manage if you can make room for their intellectual, social/emotional, and spiritual needs and then simply get out of the way as they find new and creative ways to complete their work. A new vision of the benefits of leadership will surely help you here.

Let's look at creating a coaching culture together, understanding that growing and developing talent is one of your core responsibilities in addition to getting the work done. But don't be surprised to find that if your leadership style is generating concrete results, others will likely follow. Cultures can be changed from the bottom up—all it takes is a desire and skill set to bring workers and the work they do to the next level, a kind of transformational leadership style. Let's discuss how to do just that.

THE LEADER-AS-COACH MODEL

A NEW CULTURAL CONSTRUCT
FOR TODAY'S WORKPLACE

Culture is a popular buzzword these days. It's easy to describe what a healthy culture should look like, but it's much more difficult to attain and maintain one. Culture is simply the way an organization does things in addition to what it encourages and tolerates. Culture encompasses leadership style, multigenerational inclusion, conflict resolution, ethics and morals, diversity orientation, strategic thinking, operational tactics, and so much more. When you get right down to it, though, it's an organization's style, its values, philosophy, and mission all wrapped up in one big corporate personality:

- Is your organization fun, creative, or innovative?
- Is it progressive, paternalistic, formal, or nurturing?
- Is it selfless, connected, compassionate, or judgmental?
- Is it easy to fit in or overly cliquish?
- Do staff members feel an emotional trust to management, knowing that the leadership team cares about them and their interests?

The leader-as-coach model influences culture significantly. It focuses on values held by senior and midlevel management that heavily influence the work experiences of teams and individual contributors. And although you can't change the culture of your entire organization by yourself, you have the power to create your own subculture in your department or team that influences all members' experiences of working at your company and, more important, working for you.

The leader-as-coach model creates a culture of strategic clarity, clear goals and objectives, high expectations for success, and ongoing accountability. It's based on building a relationship of trust, tapping a person's potential, building commitment, and executing goals. Coaching bases itself on the assumption that everyone can grow and that everyone has the potential to become something better, regardless of the point of departure. It focuses purposely on building trust, challenging paradigms, providing effective feedback, and listening empathically. It challenges people to reframe their point of view, find their own solutions, and set their own goals and achievement markers.

The coaching model stems from the principle of selfless leadership, in which leaders put others' needs ahead of their own and expect them to respond in kind. It accepts the premise that no job is great enough for the human spirit and asks a humble question:

How many of you believe you possess far more talent, ambition, competence, skill, and passion than your current job permits you to express?

And understanding that a majority of workers will acknowledge the limitations placed on them at work by time, resources, and—yes—their leaders' personal shortcomings or lack of engagement, selfless leadership attempts to help those being mentored to reinvent themselves, execute their predesignated goals flawlessly, and celebrate achievements and accomplishments.

I know, it sounds too good to be true. Yet, while it's not always easy to be this type of leader to your employees, it's something to strive for. It stems from your pure concern for others. It thrives on your willingness to listen, to have someone's back, and to encourage someone to be their best self—marrying both individual career interests and company interests. It's about emotional intelligence, active listening, light-handed guidance in which you ask questions more than give answers, and fun and laughter. In short, it's about otherness.

You've likely experienced this already in your career but may not have realized it. Have you ever had a favorite boss? Did you work for someone who made you feel like your opinion mattered, who challenged you to do things you didn't necessarily feel you were ready for, or who otherwise made you somehow feel special? If so, then you had an amazing coach. That person may have been your immediate supervisor, a team leader, or a department or division head, but you can be thankful that you experienced selfless leadership firsthand. And if you haven't experienced it up to this point in your career, that's unfortunate but there's always hope that you will. Remember that "bad bosses" are likewise important in our careers because they help us define who we are not. They set the outer limit for who we definitely do not wish to become. But that's not why you purchased this book. The question to ask yourself now as you continue reading is: How will you pay it forward? How will you become that person to those that follow you? Do you want to be known as a person who is excellent at growing teams, turning around flagging groups, and developing high-potential employees who may not have seen in themselves the potential that you saw in them?

Selfless leadership, emotional intelligence, and genuine care are the ingredients needed to make a coaching culture work. Never forget, the whole world is watching you. They're watching for the gift you're about to give them. Give a gift of encouragement, genuine concern, lightheartedness, and celebration. The culture of your immediate team may not be reflected company-wide, but your team will become the one that everyone wants to work on, you'll be the leader everyone wants to work for, and results will naturally follow. That's what a coaching culture creates. That's how it changes the personality of the company over time. Best of all, it can start right here, right now, as long as you're willing to be the first domino.

COACHING LEADERSHIP VERSUS TRADITIONAL MANAGEMENT

The traditional management paradigm focuses on maintaining control, making decisions, giving directives, and expecting that others will follow orders and instructions. That management model arguably worked well in environments with top-down, paternalistic structures, and fairly undereducated workforces. Many managers today still come from this school of thought, assuming that because they are managers, they know more than others and have the right and responsibility of replacing others' decisions with their own.

But today's knowledge workers are better educated, savvy users of technology, and strategic-thinking partners. The skills required for innovation and autonomous remote work no longer align with the traditional top-down management model that stifles individuality. Instead, a coaching leadership style—that focuses on developing talent and tying career and professional development interests to that of the organization—will likely garner far more significant results on a more sustainable basis.

Executive coaches exist outside companies to be hired in as consultants on a temporary basis (typically for three, six, or twelve months) to help executives become stronger leaders. The goal of executive coaching lies in building higher levels of self-mastery, self-confidence, and self-fulfillment. The coach focuses on aiding the client leader with performance achievement or a specific problem or challenge (aka performance coaching) or strengthening areas that may be otherwise holding back the executive (developmental coaching). In the first case, coaches help the executive with KPIs (key performance indicators), whereas in the second case, coaches assist in reaching particular KBIs (key behavioral indicators). The goal of the assignment is to:

- assess the situation objectively,
- help the client leader raise awareness,
- examine alternative approaches of success,
- set goals and achievement targets, and
- then gradually disengage so that new habits are formed that will sustain success without the coach's presence.

In reality, the role of an outside coach coming in to save the day is being complemented by the role of internal coaching—executives and managers focusing on many of the same things as the external executive coach but from an immediate supervisory standpoint. The internal coach and external coach share many of the same goals but likely approach the practice somewhat differently. The external coach employs a structured framework to address a client executive's challenges and development goals during the coaching process. Questions typically employed at the highest level include:

What do you want to accomplish as a result of the coaching relationship?

What legacy do you want to leave in your career?

Where do you see your "best self" five years from now, and how can I help you get there?

What are you most passionate about?

What professional and career-related opportunities are you most excited about?

On a scale of one to ten, how motivated are you to reach your goal within the time frame you've committed to?

What do you see as the best way of holding yourself accountable? How will you know when you've achieved your goal, or how will you measure success?

Moving from vision and big picture, what actions would you like to focus on over the next thirty, sixty, and ninety days?

As the relationship continues and specific performance or behavioral improvement areas are discussed, the questioning often continues like this:

How have you addressed similar situations in the past?

If you went to your most respected colleague with your problem, what would that person suggest to you?

If you saw someone else in your situation, what would you recommend?

What is another way of looking at this? What are your alternatives?

What would someone with the opposite viewpoint say?

What might possibly happen that you haven't thought about yet?

As you can see, executive coaches attempt to tease answers out of the client executives whom they coach. Their goal is to help clients find the answers within themselves by thinking the problem through to its ultimate conclusion. If the client hits a stumbling block, coaches can gently guide and sway them by asking follow-up questions that help lead the client to an alternative conclusion and go-forward strategy. In the majority of cases, clients come up with the same solution that the coach would have suggested originally; however, the coach helps them figure out that they can find those same solutions on their own.

This may all sound well and good, but how are you, as a coaching leader, expected to know how to do this? After all, you're not specifically trained or certified as an executive coach. The answer is actually fairly simple: use these same questions in your discussions with your direct reports. Create safe conditions for your team members to find their own solutions. Hold back from giving answers and learn to question others to their own truths in an effort to build their self-confidence and managerial competency. In short, create your own structured framework to approach your staff members' challenges and development goals.

Ah, but you don't have time for this, you say, and even if you wanted to, when would you do it? Again, a simple answer: set time aside to help your employees establish and monitor their own goals. Then have them set up quarterly meetings with you so that they can share their progress toward their goals. We'll talk more about goal setting and quarterly check-in meetings later in the book, but for now, just know that it's totally within your scope of control to:

- ▦ help individuals shift paradigms that limit their progress,
- ▦ increase self-awareness and allow for transformational change,
- ▦ help individuals find their voice, set their own goals, and suggest their own solutions when they encounter problems, and
- ▦ transform careers and even people's lives to a higher state of meaning, purpose, and fulfillment.

All you have to do is care. Simply demonstrate curiosity and true concern and allow employees to find their own way, whether in day-to-day operations or in quarterly and annual review meetings. Practice whole-person leadership, meaning that you demonstrate concern for the physical, emotional, mental, and spiritual needs of those you serve as a leader. And always remember that change—*real* change—comes from the inside out, not the outside in. Allow others to assume responsibility and accountability for themselves. Don't give them a fish; teach them to fish. You can give no greater gift to those you influence.

EXERCISE

Think about the last time someone coached you in a way that stuck and made a difference, when the focus was on helping you learn, improve, and grow. How did it make you feel? Did it seem so elusive that you felt you'd never be able to do that for someone else? Of course not. Kindness is the quickest way to workplace success. Simply lead with kindness and authenticity. Anyone who tells you otherwise or that the workplace consists only of sharks or bullies is likely not the person you want to mentor you in the fine art of coaching leadership.

3

EMPLOYEE ENGAGEMENT
A CRITICAL STARTING POINT

I f there's one hallmark of a coaching culture that you'll want to start with, it's overall employee engagement. The primary drivers of employee engagement include recognition, career development, and the relationship with your immediate manager. There are others, of course: job content and challenge, relationships with your peers, resources and budget, and the like. But if you generally want to capture your corporate culture in just a few words, look no further than the degree to which communication and recognition are open, employees' professional and personal needs are prioritized, and strong relationships with immediate supervisors are built on trust.

How can you, as a frontline manager, move the needle in terms of positively affecting the level of employee engagement on your team? First, understand that American companies spend close to $10 billion per year on programs, software, and apps to boost employee engagement, but many US workers would say they don't make a significant difference. Why not? Because they're not personal. The relationship with your boss drives engagement—it's real, it's palpable, and it either leaves you feeling like that individual has your back or else you need to somehow protect yourself from that person. (In the latter case, employee engagement likely is at a minimum.)

Next, it's important to realize that employee engagement is owned by employees themselves—not by their managers. You are not responsible for motivating anyone: motivation is internal, and you can't motivate me any more than I can motivate you. But as a leader, you *are* responsible for creating an environment in which people can motivate themselves. That may sound like a subtle difference, but it's actually profound: all development is self-development. Your company can offer the best training programs, cross-training opportunities, tuition reimbursement benefits to garner additional certifications and licenses, and much more, but those programs won't help an individual learn, grow, or advance in her career if she isn't motivated to take advantage of them.

To truly affect the sense of engagement experienced by your workers, consider doing the following (which we'll explore later in this book):

■ Conduct "stay interviews" to ensure your top performers are fully engaged in their work and recognized for a job well done.

■ Challenge your superstars to assume greater responsibilities within the organization, especially in terms of assuming roles as ambassadors, buddies, and teacher/trainers.

■ Offer to help your team members update their resumes and LinkedIn profiles, codifying their achievements in terms of increased revenue, decreased expenses, or saved time.

- Develop stretch assignments for moderate-performing employees who may be ready to step up to new opportunities as they arise.
- Encourage acquisition of new technical and software skills that will help people prepare for their next move in career progression.
- Rotate assignments so employees can "test drive" working in other departments for two weeks (or for several hours per day over a two-week period).

There are many more examples, of course, that will be unique to your environment. In the broadest spirit, treat your employees as trusted partners. Encourage people to learn and grow, to feel comfortable in their skin, and to come always from gratitude.

Recognize as well, however, that for some, career growth and development may not meet their current needs. Instead, work-life balance and flexibility may be more important at any given time, depending on the individual's personal or family situation. Others may not possess the ambition level to pursue stretch assignments or acquire new skills, opting instead to stick with their current role and responsibilities. Coaching leadership isn't intended only to make people want to grow more personally and professionally: it helps people experience greater acceptance at work, teaching them to look internally for their own answers and solutions and to feel confident that they are doing their best work every day.

Engagement and personal fulfillment, as it turns out, take on many forms. Allow for that. You need a mixture of racehorses and plow horses: racehorses often take home the prize but can run only in short sprints. Plow horses rarely perform with distinction, but you can count on them to deliver, quarter after quarter and year after year. Coaching leadership makes it safe for people to find their balance. Engagement shows itself in a level of emotional commitment and connection that employees have to their boss, their teammates, and your organization. Engagement is driven by how successful they are at work and in their personal lives. Engagement captures the spirit, energy, and discretionary effort that people put into their work, and it magnifies your success as a leader when your team reflects the peace and wisdom that emanates from you. Create and enable greater individual success, and higher engagement will then follow. One thing's for sure: the high degree of appreciation and trust that you model will repay itself in kind. What comes from you always returns to you in some shape or form. That's simply the law of the universe. Use it wisely to your advantage.

4

IDENTIFYING HIGH-POTENTIAL TALENT TO DEVELOP YOUR LEADERSHIP BENCH

Selfless leadership focuses on replacing yourself within your organization. I know that might sound counterintuitive, but in its highest sense, you're preparing your direct reports for their next move in career progression, which, as your organization chart likely reveals, is your position. That's nothing to be concerned about—it's simply a matter of perspective. Helping others get ahead in their careers to replace you is the ultimate gift you give your company. After all, it speaks to your outstanding leadership abilities if your organization wouldn't skip a beat if you were temporarily incapacitated or even suddenly left.

Sounds good in theory, but many of us won't quite go that far for fear of either losing our jobs or being replaced by those up-and-comers below us, right? Well, yes and no: while many of us sense some level of insecurity about building a team so strong that we could fall off the planet and be immediately replaced, there's more to it than that. Growing your people doesn't have to be a threat; it can be seen as an amazing opportunity. For, as you grow strong teams, you'll be earmarked as a talent developer, a team turnaround specialist, and someone who can clearly take on more responsibility. That prevents you from being stuck at one level or one position and frees you up to grow and promote in your career. Even if promotion isn't your ultimate goal, think of how proud you would be of yourself when a member of your team thanks you years later for being the best boss they ever had and attributes their success to your mentorship.

How do you identify those individuals in your department or on your team who are ready to promote now? First, you can hold what are known as "calibration" exercises with your boss and peers to assess talent readiness. This is usually done as the organization gears up for annual performance reviews. For example, the head of human resources calls a meeting with her direct reports—the heads of recruitment, employee relations, compensation and benefits, training and talent development, employee relations, and the like—asking them to discuss their individual teams with the rest of the leadership group. Everyone has an opportunity to discuss their experiences with each member of the extended team with the hopes of identifying the top players who are ready for more responsibility across the entire department.

This is usually accomplished with the help of what's known as a "9-box" tool, where individual names are placed according to performance and potential. A simple 9-box diagram looks like this:

SUCCESSION PLANNING ORGANIZATIONAL REVIEW

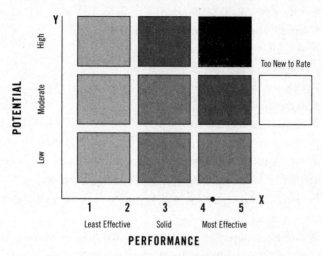

Talent is assigned according to leadership team agreement, and the goal then becomes to find special ways of developing those in the upper far right quadrant. It's the core idea behind succession planning and creates a healthy competition among group heads who lobby to get their people ranked as close to the top right ("high potential, high performance") as possible.

Second, whether you employ a 9-box succession planning tool or not, you can conduct talent-calibration sessions by grading potential leaders in the following categories and determining if they truly are ready to step up now. If not, you can likewise discuss how much time they'll need before they're ready to be promoted into specific roles to replace you or another member of the management team in the future:

- achievement and accomplishment record
- teambuilding skills/peer trust
- judgment and decision-making
- diversity orientation, openness, and respect
- customer satisfaction and loyalty
- adaptability and change management
- communication and listening skills
- technical skills and acumen
- creativity and innovation

There are many competencies, of course, and these are in no particular order. Much depends on your organizational goals and priorities, which are likewise reviewed at the beginning of such meetings.

What's most important is that you understand how these calibration exercises tie into your succession planning and annual performance review processes: you're constantly identifying, honing, and developing talent. You make people development a core part of your organizational culture. You set up people for greater success, whether high performers or middle performers, which we'll cover in the next section. (Note that low performers are addressed in book 4 of the *Paul Falcone Workplace Leadership Series*, titled *Leadership Defense*.)

Overall, though, you want to make sure your team can operate fully without you. Get into that habit early in your leadership career because it's a healthy, selfless mindset that will help you establish your reputation as a great talent developer. By the way, whoever tends to dominate the 9-box game in terms of developing the most future leaders is often the person earmarked to replace the department head. Calibration, succession planning, and annual performance reviews all tie in beautifully together when done right, and they provide you with an outstanding opportunity to demonstrate your people- and leadership skills.

MOVING THE MIDDLE

A SMART APPROACH TO TEAM DEVELOPMENT

Per the Gallup Organization and others, roughly 30 percent of workers describe themselves as "fully engaged" in their work and doing their best work possible on a regular basis. About 50 percent describe themselves as "somewhat disengaged," meaning that they go through the motions of their job, but their hearts really aren't into it. In other words, they're not necessarily putting forward their best efforts or going above or beyond. Worse, almost a full 20 percent admit to being "actively disengaged," meaning they're actively looking for other work or otherwise purposely exhibiting behaviors that are counterproductive to the goals of the organization. While no workplace will ever achieve 100 percent employee commitment, the questions remain:

- How do you leverage the top 30 percent and groom them for growth and additional responsibilities?
- How do you address the bottom 20 percent who not only lag personally but often serve as a net negative to the rest of the team's overall productivity and performance?

■ And most important, how do you address the middle 50 percent that perform consistently but not necessarily with distinction? If you could "move the middle" by influencing and developing that cohort's muscle, wouldn't that likely have the biggest impact of all? And is there a way that the top 30 percent could be leveraged to serve as role models and positive career influencers for the middle 50 percent? Likewise, what would it look like on your team or in your department to transition to this leadership approach and make it your own?

In reality, in most organizations, the top 20–30 percent got there on their own. Because of their smarts, personalities, strong work ethic, or ambition, they placed themselves in a position to excel in their careers. Retaining and developing that talent is crucial. It's a sad fact, however, that most companies spend most of their time and effort tending to the bottom 20 percent, crafting policies that address over-the-line conduct, disciplining, terminating, and laying off individuals and teams that are not contributing properly or otherwise holding their own.

Ah, but the middle 50 percent. They're usually ignored. They do their work, day in and day out, without complaining. They contribute consistently but often without distinction. They work to live rather than live to work, and while that's not necessarily a bad thing, they present tremendous potential that often goes untapped. After all, they're not necessarily winning the employee-of-the-month or employee-of-the-year awards, as the top 30 percent are. And they're not constantly in and out of human resources with complaints, requiring tough conversations, team interventions, and documented warnings, like the bottom 20 percent. No, this "middle earth" group may be where the greatest impact and your greatest opportunity can be found. It's likely where you'll get the biggest return on investment in terms of your leadership efforts. And it's where you have the strongest opportunity to grow people from the middle to the top cohort, all because of your exceptional leadership, communication, and teambuilding capabilities.

The key question is, how do you get them there? How do you keep the top 30 percent motivated and experiencing the highest level of Maslow's hierarchy (where they experience true fulfillment and career satisfaction) while encouraging and prodding the middle 50 percent to join the ranks of the top 30 percent? The answer: by spiking employee engagement. Employee engagement has become the holy grail in the management of human capital talent. Employee engagement is the alignment of individual and organizational goals and values to better drive both business results and personal aspirations. It combines the individual's intrinsic career and professional interests (personal gain) with the organization's growth and development goals (company gain) so that hearts are pierced, true believers are created, and real discretionary effort is turned on. As we move through this book, let's review our strategies for employee engagement and high performance and productivity for the top 30 percent and the middle 50 percent, with the goal of moving select members of the middle group to the top. That's a noble approach and will likely help you become someone's favorite boss and mentor over time—an admirable goal that works for you, for them, and most important, for your organization.

ARE YOU A COACHABLE LEADER?

ASSESSING YOUR OWN LEADERSHIP STYLE

A coachable leader possesses the following characteristics:

- leads by example/demonstrates role model leadership
- demonstrates high standards of ethics and fairness
- places the needs of staff above his or her own
- provides adequate structure, direction, and feedback to subordinates
- ensures open communication and staff camaraderie
- recognizes and rewards staff achievements
- encourages staff members to assume responsibility for their actions
- listens actively and with empathy
- allocates resources effectively in the face of competing demands
- creates a culture of mutual trust and caring
- channels strategic vision into concrete plans of action
- consistently earns respect from subordinates
- holds him- or herself accountable for staff performance

- ■ readily shares information and develops staff by delegating to their strengths
- ■ provides strategic vision of future goals and objectives
- ■ develops practical action plans for achieving goals and objectives
- ■ takes appropriate risks and encourages others to do so
- ■ makes high-probability decisions even when he or she doesn't have all the facts

There are many leadership tools to help you gauge your personal management style, in terms of how well you communicate, hold others accountable, motivate and develop your staff, manage conflict, and develop other skills. You can find such assessments on the internet, and many of them are free; however, the following five questions provide a brief version you can use right now. As a certified executive coach, I'm qualified to partner with you on this activity, so let's have some fun with it.

How you reflect on the following questions will provide you with some interesting insights about your leanings and proclivities that you may want to ponder. There are no right or wrong answers here; likewise, there's no judgment. These are simple self-reflection questions that I typically ask when in a coaching capacity; you may want to think about these as you continue to grow in your career as well. Consider implementing action plans around any objective and dispassionate responses that you're not comfortable with or want to change.

Question 1: Would you want to work for you? This question is actually a series of mini questions; answer them honestly:

- ■ What kind of boss would you be to work for on a daily basis?

- Would you feel motivated to come to work and do your best work every day?
- To what degree would others describe you as a selfless leader?

Question 2: What are three adjectives your most respected critic might use to describe you as a business professional and as a leader? Again, you can break this down into a series of questions:

- Would the words *honest, ethical,* and *transparent* come immediately to mind?
- What could you add or subtract to your leadership and management style that would garner a greater sense of loyalty among those you work with and lead?
- What adjectives would you use in defining the best boss you've ever had?
- How close would you say you are to becoming that person to the people you work with and supervise every day?

Question 3: How do people finish the sentence: I know [YOUR NAME HERE]. He's / She's . . . Be careful. The second half of this sentence represents your equity and total worth to any organization, present or future. Much like the questions above, it represents your sum-total contribution to those around you and your impact on them and on your organization. Your reputation is your most important asset. A sixty-second elevator pitch can capture your entire contributions and personality in an instant.

Spend time with this particular question and complete the sentence as objectively and impartially as you can. It could be well worth your time and something worth sharing with your boss or someone you trust who could mentor and coach you through improving your self-described reputation. After all, coaching is all about building self-awareness and capitalizing on your strengths while muting certain recognized limitations.

Question 4: How would you self-assess your leadership skills? Here's an exercise with which you can grade yourself now and follow up over time to assess areas where you're building ethical and leadership muscle versus areas that may be suffering from a lack of attention. On a scale of one to ten, with ten being the highest, how would you grade yourself in the following areas:

1. Your overall career progression to date: _____

_____

_____

_____

2. Your role within and contribution to your current company: _____

_____

_____

_____

3. The trust level you have with your immediate manager at work: _____

_____

_____

_____

4. Your perception for ethics, morals, and fairness: _____

_____

_____

_____

5. The level or degree of trust your employees would have in divulging something to you that could make them feel vulnerable: _____

6. Your relationship with your peers as someone who keeps their word, can be relied on to maintain confidentiality, and who is known for loyalty and having others' backs:

7. How close to "role-model status" you would grade your leadership, communication, and teambuilding skills:

8. Relative to the best boss you've ever had, you are that type of leader to the people you currently supervise: _____

Notice how questions 1–3 above may influence your responses to questions 4–8 that follow. That's because how you feel about yourself often influences how you lead and manage others. If you're fully satisfied with your career and your role within your current organization and have a healthy relationship with your boss, then your own leadership style tends to benefit as you pass those good feelings and peace of mind along to those you work with and supervise every day. Conversely, if you find yourself feeling stymied at work, treading water career-wise, or otherwise feeling challenged by your relationship with your immediate supervisor, it could detract from being the best leader you could be to others.

Again, there's no right or wrong here: simply an observation of how various influences impact our day-to-day leadership style. What's important is that you see this objectively and choose to be the best and most ethical boss you can be, despite any limitations that may be challenging you personally.

Question 5: If the whole organization followed your lead, would you be happy with where you took it? Now *there's* a question that should get your attention! Leaders often fall into self-defense mode, arguing, "Well, at least I don't . . ." and expect that to somehow justify their behaviors. Likewise, they simply write off any shortcomings brought to their attention by validating, "That's just the way I am." Finally, some launch into a preemptive strike by complaining about how their bosses treat them: "Would you like me to tell you what Jonathan said to me just before this meeting, Paul? Would you like me to give a little sampling of how he *treats me with dignity and respect*? It's not fair that I get mistreated like that day in and day out, while you tell me I've got to become and remain a role model leader for my employees. You can't have it both ways."

To a degree, that logic is absolutely correct. What goes around comes around, and when one senior leader strips people of their dignity, engages in public shaming sessions, or plays mental games on their direct reports, it can warp reality and make it difficult for you (or any one of your peers) to position yourself as a model boss to your own employees. That being said, I repeat: you get to choose the reality you wish to experience—maybe not whenever you're with your supervisor, but certainly whenever you're with your team or family and friends.

Don't give up hope. Look inward for the courage, humility, and discipline you need to excel even under these conditions. Most important, teach what you choose to learn, calm and heal the room, and remember that no one does anything wrong, given their model of the world. You are not your boss. You have the power to help your employees experience a totally different reality, despite the challenges you may face from time to time under someone who may not be a particularly healthy person or leader. Leading with ethics and morals is never beyond your grasp, lest you believe it so. The question once again is, *who are you and who do you choose to be?* Always be the cause of your experiences. Always remember the leader you were meant to be.

PERFORMANCE MANAGEMENT

REAL-TIME FEEDBACK, QUARTERLY GOAL CHECK-INS, AND ANNUAL REPORTS

B efore we launch into this chapter, let's address the elephant in the room. Everyone hates performance reviews! Managers hate giving them. Employees hate receiving them. Employment lawyers worry about their codifying an employee's acceptable performance or behavior after the company terminated the individual for cause. Hence, the "abolish performance appraisals" movement is alive and well. Why? Because measuring human productivity and potential is difficult. Social scientists, academics, consulting firms, and others come up with new structures, programs, software platforms, and social media tools to replace the traditional performance review system, which is described as outdated, broken, limited, and the like.

In contrast, they pose that today's most successful companies are transforming their old-fashioned, one-way feedback processes into dynamic, collaborative systems that apply the latest social technologies to employee feedback and recognition. Instead of a onetime annual evaluation of performance, managers and employees receive collective feedback from everyone across the company, thereby generating more accurate, actionable results than traditional methods. Employees get to recognize one another's great work on a daily basis, managers aren't left to their own devices to render judgment on someone's historical contribution to the organization over the past year, and voilà—social recognition creates employee satisfaction, energy, and even happiness in the company—leading to the ultimate goal of employee engagement.

And you know what? They're all correct! There is no right or wrong way to assess people. And employing new, groundbreaking performance management systems and social recognition solutions often work well in redefining how companies understand, manage, and motivate their employees. Yet there's one caveat, and it's important: software tools will never replace human interaction and communication. Recognition is meant to be personal. No app—no matter how many positive hits you receive—can replace your manager acknowledging you in front of the rest of the senior leadership team for a job well done. Don't fall prey to thinking that you can delegate recognition and engagement to software or an app. They can help, no doubt, but all recognition and engagement stems from personal relationships. Besides, in practice, people rarely share negative information via an app, and if they do, that will likely trigger a public shaming event and the immediate need to bring everyone together in person to heal wounds, hurt feelings, and embarrassment, whether inflicted intentionally or unintentionally.

Yes, it's easy to find multiple shortcomings with the annual performance review system, but if we tweak it, it can work brilliantly. When done right, your organization's performance management program captures annual contributions, incorporates goals, and projects areas for personal and professional development. The performance management cycle aligns individuals' professional goals with the organization's business objectives. Performance touch-base meetings highlight employee growth and goal achievement, pinpoint important training opportunities, and drive higher engagement and productivity through recognition and celebration. Frequent and goal-driven individual development plans (IDPs) focus on supporting employees to reach preestablished goals and key performance indicators (KPIs) and provide opportunities for constructive feedback along the way.

Your organization's performance management program should:

1. provide frequent feedback, and
2. focus on inspiring future performance improvement.

It's that simple. Ensuring that these two boxes are consistently checked is the litmus test to ensure you're heading in the right direction. Instead of revealing "annual surprises" and often disappointing feedback, reviews—quarterly and annual—become more accurate measurements of employee progress, more relevant trackers of each employee's impact on the organization, and an ongoing discussion to address future growth and professional development. Said another way, your organization's performance management program becomes the glue that binds employees to the organization and to their mentor supervisors, not a year-end stressor that both managers and employees wish they could avoid.

And yes, this can work consistently across your entire organization, as it does in some of the strongest and most well-known companies in corporate America. There's no reason you can't incorporate a true performance management mindset in your department or on your team. You simply need to make it a priority, discuss what it should look and feel like with your team, and shift the responsibility for career and professional development to your team members—where it rightfully belongs—so that you can serve appropriately as their mentor and coach.

So, when considering the types of tools that you use for employee feedback, think *both-and*, not *either-or*. There's more than enough room in our universe to include new tools, systems, and methodologies. Let's clearly focus, however, on how to provide feedback, how often, and in what context. You can use all the e-tools you want to supplement the annual review but not to supplant it. Much like Wall Street's approach to assessing the performance of publicly traded companies, quarterly and annual reviews will and should remain the staple for employee feedback and recognition. Let us show you how, especially in terms of the types of questions that drive such quarterly and annual meetings, in the pages ahead.

LIMITATIONS OF HISTORIC PERFORMANCE REVIEW SYSTEMS

When you begin discussions about performance management, your mind likely takes you to the concepts of *performance appraisal* and *performance review*, and rightfully so. At the core of every performance management system lies the document of documents, the Grand Poobah of administrivia, the feared emblem of management incompetence from the TV show *The Office*—the annual review. And maybe those indictments are deserved. Performance management systems, whether human or electronic, suffer from their ability to capture an entire year's work, efforts, projects, time commitments, and so much more.

As an author and human resources executive, I would have to agree that old-school performance appraisal isn't working. In survey after survey, managers dislike issuing them because they feel more like an unnecessary chore and less like a tool for meaningful change in performance and achievements. Workers dislike receiving them because of the critical nature of once-a-year feedback, which tends to focus more on shortcomings than on celebrating successes. Further, few employees state they feel inspired to improve their performance after receiving an annual review.

More specifically, historical paper-based annual performance reviews suffer from myriad shortcomings like:

- bearing a single point of failure (that is, the supervisor's gut feeling, predisposition, or whim)
- capturing a narrow range of information, often influenced by what is known as "recency bias"
- lacking objectivity or quantitative proof of assessment
- measuring only a small subset of employee behaviors

New technologies will make enterprise-wide performance reviews easier to scale and more consistent, capturing crowdsourced feedback and trends and patterns from multiple stakeholders throughout the year. And with all those advantages, assessing human performance will still be a difficult challenge. Easier in some respects but challenging nevertheless.

It's important that we understand the broad goals of any performance management system:

- ensuring that a set of activities and outputs meets an organization's goals in an effective and efficient manner
- focusing on the performance of an organization, a department, an employee, or the processes in place to manage particular tasks
- furthering the continuous process of improving performance by setting individual and team goals that are aligned to the strategic goals of the organization

▦ aligning performance to achieve organizational goals, reviewing and assessing progress, and developing the knowledge, skills, and abilities of the workers who perform them

You get the idea. Anything that attempts to capture overall employee performance over an entire year can rightfully be described as an "annual performance review."

But what exactly is *performance management*? Is it a record based on quality, quantity, or both? Does it encompass behavior and conduct? Should attendance and tardiness (that is, reliability) be captured, especially in light of the many leave laws that protect workers from scrutiny of any kind? Performance management at its highest level is all about accurately evaluating employees' proficiency and improvement over time. Defining performance, however, remains a challenge for any organization, not only in terms of its structure, market, and competitive needs but also in terms of its mission, vision, and values.

As we'll see throughout this chapter, how an organization defines performance and conduct makes a key difference in the type of feedback that each employee receives at annual review time. Our goal in this chapter will be to ratchet up performance expectations, assess goal achievement, and set future goals within the annual performance review setting. More specifically, we'll review the performance review cycle with the following annual rhythm:

Phase 1: Goal setting and planning (beginning of review year)

Phase 2: Ongoing real-time feedback and coaching (throughout the review year)

Phase 3: Appraisal and reward (at the conclusion of the review year)

Each phase logically flows into the other in an unending cycle of sorts, where the appraisal and reward process (phase 3) continues directly into the goal-setting and planning (phase 1) stage for the upcoming year. The system is designed to provide continuous improvement feedback, allowing for the individual to redirect his efforts and energies to gain the greatest advantage for the company and, in doing so, to strengthen his resume and career progression potential.

The biggest problem with a system like this is that phases 1 and 2 barely get addressed during a typical worker's tenure. Ongoing feedback and the space to discuss performance improvement, along with career and professional development, get short shrift in an environment where production demands seem never ending and managers find it challenging to provide constructive feedback. Instead, only phase 3 gets addressed once a year—checking a box on the manager's to-do list that permits the employee to receive a merit increase or bonus. That's what has to change, and that's what makes annual reviews so despised. In many organizations, the entire process is reduced to a paper chase—a mere formality that typically underwhelms the employee, often surprises the individual to the downside, and then gets filed away in a cabinet drawer, never to see the light of day again. Yuck! Let's reinvent the performance management process the way it's intended to serve us—paying special attention to phases 1 and 2 so that phase 3 poses no surprises, few disappointments, and ample opportunity to celebrate.

8

CREATING AN ACHIEVEMENT MINDSET
GOAL SETTING AND PROGRESS MEASUREMENT

T here are several rules that make it easy and effective to craft just the right goals for each of your team members. Start by creating three goals: one pertaining to the company, another to your department, and a third to a personal endeavor that makes good career sense for your employee and also benefits the organization. If your company doesn't establish goals, then simply work with two. And if your organization or department doesn't set goals, then work with your team members in creating two to three personal / professional / career goals each.

Meaningful goals keep your team's eye on the bigger picture, keep you all working in alignment, and translate well to each team member's resume and LinkedIn profile. That's right—get them thinking about their own professional and career development so they can map their achievements on paper and use it at self-review time (which we'll cover shortly) and for their own personal benefit.

Next, make sure your team creates SMART goals—Specific, Measurable, Attainable, Realistic, and Time-Bound. In fact, let's add one more M—Meaningful. Goals should excite employees:

completing a degree, gaining a certification, broadening their technical skill set, achieving something at work that can be documented and move their career forward—that's how you assist employees in creating exciting goals that are meaningful to them career wise. That's also why each employee should be involved in creating his or her own personal goals: shared company/department goals and personal goals make up the right mix when it comes time to the annual goal-setting exercise.

For a goal to be achievable, it has to be personal and meaningful to the employee. (That's the main reason why employees should be asked to codevelop their goals rather than simply be assigned goals.) They should be:

■ challenging: think "just out of reach" or "stretch goals";
■ measurable: demonstrated either by a quantifiable benchmark or a qualitative description as a determinant of success; and
■ time-bound: with a specific deadline associated with them.

What is most important, however, is that there must be a plan for periodic measurement and review. Goals are not intended to be static; dynamic goals need to be reviewed and honed over time. The likelihood of achievement goes way up using this framework of employee involvement and periodic review.

Further, linking last year's goals to this year's performance review is a natural outcome of organizational growth and progress. "Individual development plans" (IDPs) stem from one-on-one goal-setting exercises between you and your subordinates that move their career along and also benefit the organization. You'll likely review each employee's IDP four times per year: once per quarter leading up to annual performance review time. For example, if you use a calendar year and pay merit increases and bonuses in January based on the prior year's performance, the rhythm of the IDP review might look like this:

Annual Review and IDP/Goal Setting: December
Quarter 1 IDP Review: March
Quarter 2 IDP Review: June
Quarter 3 IDP Review: September

This natural rhythm permits you to discuss progress toward goals at your quarterly one-on-one meetings, any unforeseen roadblocks coming your way, necessary pivots, and occasionally goal amendments to better reflect your company's, department's, or personal changes in plan. After the quarter 3 IDP review, it's time for your self-evaluation and then annual performance review. Just like the stock market requires publicly traded companies to report quarterly performance that leads up to its annual report, employee performance requires check-ins and updates at regular intervals. It's caring, it's personal, and it means a lot to employees to know their manager and company invest in them this way.

Next, make sure that you're reviewing the past few years' reviews with the employee before setting goals. That's because you may just find that the employee has the same goal year after year and never really reaches it. In those cases, it's time to reassess those old, tired goals and refresh and replace them with something more realistic and obtainable or move the conversation in a different direction altogether in terms of the individual's inability to meet historic goals. More important, if SMART and meaningful goals are selected by the employee and not met, there's clearly something wrong that needs to be addressed, potentially from a progressive disciplinary standpoint. But when it's done right, addressing last year's goals in formatting this year's target areas will demonstrate a clear connection or nexus among goals that overlap and move the needle forward from year to year in terms of personal and professional development.

Finally, focus on building an achievement mentality among your team members by helping them quantify results whenever possible. Just as resumes typically include dollars and percentages to demonstrate true improvement, IDPs and annual self-evaluations should do the same. It's not always easy to quantify the impact of your team's efforts—you may need the help of finance, sales, or legal to do so. But the more you quantify results, the more meaningful the exercise becomes.

Looking for ideas to spur team and individual goals? Share some of the following questions with your team and see if you can come to a group consensus in terms of what's important and what should be pursued goal-wise:

Company Goals (set by corporate)

What opportunities may we be missing that will provide us with a clear advantage over the short- or long term?

Who are our biggest competitors in the marketplace? What are they doing that's working for them that we could incorporate?

What patterns and trends appear to threaten our business, and how can we get out ahead of it?

What is our reputation on Glassdoor.com and other culture and career websites that address our organization as a best place to work?

Department Goals

What are the three biggest obstacles our department is facing in terms of building a stronger reputation among our clients or getting higher customer satisfaction scores?

How effective are we at cross-training one another and building talent supply across all key areas of our department so that we avoid "single point of failure" syndrome when someone is out ill?

Is our turnover rate acceptable? More important, how well are we promoting and backfilling positions internally rather than constantly having to look externally for new talent?

Individual Goals

Individual goals tie career and professional development to the organization's needs so that both are in harmony. Examples include:

- acquisition of licenses, certifications, or technical skills;

- opportunities to build up areas we don't particularly like—for example, public speaking or business writing;

- opportunities to expand one's professional network by joining a local business association or network;

- exposure to other parts of the organization via half-day or one- or two-week rotational assignments, and the like.

The possibilities are endless. What's important is that your employees are dedicated to their goals and IDPs and that you create the space for them quarterly to discuss and refine them. That's what career and professional development are all about.

NOTE TO SELF

You would be surprised how many employees complain that "No one ever gives me any feedback" or "You never hear of a job well done around here, but make one mistake, and they're all over you." Be careful not to call attention only to the negative or "lead by error." It happens more often that you think, and it's easy to fix by simply shifting responsibility for feedback to the staff members themselves. Quarterly IDP reviews are scheduled by employees, and they are responsible for preparing all the content and suggestions. Your job, at that point, is to serve as mentor and coach. It's a simple shift in paradigm that eliminates complaints of "no feedback" or "little communication" because you'll have assigned responsibility for scheduling the meetings to the employees themselves. That's treating people like adults and establishing proactive work habits for your team members— something they will likely thank you for as you demonstrate role-model leadership behavior for them to emulate.

THE WAY FORWARD

REAL-TIME FEEDBACK

Arguably, the biggest shortcoming in the field of annual performance reviews is stale data. Managers are accused of assigning grades haphazardly based on gut impressions with little evidence to prove their point.

There are two ways to overcome this persistent challenge:

1. A Critical Incident Diary helps you capture specific events at particular dates and times that you can refer to during your quarterly IDP reviews and annual performance reviews.
2. Real-time feedback permits you to share kudos and concerns at the time they occur—not weeks or months later.

Wait—there's an app for that! In fact, there are many. Social media and new technologies permit organizations like yours to share feedback on an ongoing basis throughout the review year. As such, feedback apps also increase employee engagement because people enjoy getting real-time feedback as much as possible—as long as it's positive. Which is both the strength and weakness of such media: they're great for giving pats on the back, but they're not particularly well designed for delivering negative feedback. In fact, if negative information needs to be shared, it should always be done in person and not electronically (including via mouse-to-mouse combat in an email). So yes—if your organization enjoys tech gadgets and is looking to increase employee engagement, invest in an app that allows for peer recognition, gamification, awards, and the like. But always remember that computers can't replace the human touch, especially when dealing with matters that can hurt feelings or spur confrontations.

Critical Incident Diaries are simply folders that you retain for each of your direct reports:

■ Drop in notes from satisfied customers.
■ Record any outstanding work performed by the employee throughout the year or quarter so that you can make solid reference to it in the future.
■ And yes, retain it for negative information as well, including customer complaints and written warnings.

But there's one huge disadvantage to such folders: if the information isn't shared with the employee at the time it occurs, then retaining the paperwork is practically useless. The information is relevant only if it's discussed with the employee *at the time*— whether positive, negative, instructive, constructive, or the like. The data can't be stored for months and then sprung on the employee at a later date, demonstrating and justifying the point you're trying to make as a manager. The rule "document, document, document" has severe limitations: the documentation is relevant only if it's shared with the employee at the time it happens. It can then be added to a quarterly IDP meeting or annual review as a reminder or historical record of what was discussed at the time.

Regarding real-time feedback, it sure would be great to delegate that to an app—especially if the feedback is negative. In reality, though, it can be difficult for managers to share difficult feedback with their employees on the spot. Make it easier to share uncomfortable news by following the rule we learned in the second grade: it's not what you say, it's how you say it that counts. Delivering good news is fun, easy, motivational, and engaging; providing real-time negative feedback can be daunting, intimidating, and nerve racking, to say the least. This isn't exactly a "be careful what you ask for," but know that delivering feedback in real time—whether positive or negative—is a skill you need to hone throughout your career.

Some managers rarely give positive feedback when something great occurs. Big mistake. People thrive on recognition and appreciation. Many managers rarely provide constructive feedback when something negative occurs—another big mistake. Providing real-time feedback isn't easy at times, and no app in the world will be able to replace the personal discomfort of sharing negative news. Just know that when it comes to career and professional development, you would be doing those whom you serve a disservice by not raising their awareness of certain achievements or shortcomings. Praise in public; censure in private. But always have enough respect for your team members that you share and celebrate what they're doing right while holding them accountable and teaching them when opportunities to do so arise.

NOTE

Conflict is inevitable; relational combat is optional.

There are three forms of fighting that are considered relational killers:

- Absolutes: "I'm right, you're wrong"; egos

- Blame: "It's all your fault"; places accountability elsewhere

- Character attack: "You are irresponsible"

Don't let your real-time feedback devolve into a blame game, void of accountability. Yes, people can become defensive, and conflict can escalate when providing feedback that is considered negative or potentially adversarial. But person-to-person dialogue makes for safe conversations. Dialogue is required for conflict, and negative or constructive feedback should not be delivered by app, email, or any other form of electronic media because it is void of context and social clues. In fact, many bosses never become true leaders because they fail to master the communication framework for addressing challenges constructively. When it comes to delivering challenging feedback, always invite conversation and input, acknowledge and clarify throughout, and do your genuine best to reach a mutual understanding or agreement with a personal touch.

10

QUARTERLY REPORTS AND CHECK-INS
COACHING WINDOWS OF OPPORTUNITY

I believe one of the reasons quarterly touch-base meetings often don't occur is because frontline leaders aren't sure what to talk about. Following is a short list of coaching questions that can be expanded over time. These are meant to spur a conversation, engage the employee, and build trust and rapport over time:

What would you like to discuss today? Have you prepared anything you'd like me to review first (your resume, productivity spreadsheets, graphs, charts, tables)?

What's changed since the last time we met like this?

How do you feel you're doing performance-wise? Do you feel you're doing your best work every day? What could we do differently to support you more?

Let's take a look at your IDP together. How are you progressing toward your goals?

Have you faced any unforeseen roadblocks? Do you see a pivot coming either in terms of your goals, priorities, or what you're focusing on?

Are you on target to meet your quarterly and/or annual goals?

What can we quantify in terms of increased revenue, decreased expenses, or saved time?

How can I help you in terms of providing the right amount of structure, direction, and feedback throughout the quarter?

From a coaching or mentoring standpoint, what can I do to support you further in terms of professional and career development?

As openly as you'd be comfortable sharing, what could I do differently to support our team at a higher level?

Who on the team is your greatest supporter? Is there anyone you'd describe as a detractor?

On a scale of one to ten, how strong would you say we perform as a department, especially in terms of delivering on our goals and objectives? (Why are we an [eight]? What would make us a ten?)

Do you feel the team has your back?

Do you have any recommendations for senior management in terms of communication style and frequency? Do you understand what the organization is all about or do you sense a disconnect?

Have any of your career or professional goals changed? Is there anything you want to add or subtract from your goal list to make this exercise more relevant?

Do you feel your career and professional development needs are being met? Is there anything I can do differently to help you build your resume or LinkedIn profile?

As far as the measurable and tangible outcomes you've identi-fied to demonstrate that you're meeting your goals, how are you doing?

If you could add one thing to our performance or culture as a department or team, what might that be?

If you could choose one thing to focus on during our next IDP meeting in about three months, what might that be?

Some questions will depend on your industry, business, and the types of direct reports on your team. For example, some employees may want to learn a foreign language, get published, or have a chance to visit the corporate parent company over-seas. Others may want to cross-train in a different discipline to gain a pay differential and increase their hourly pay rate. Some may want to become associated with your organization's high-potential program, while others may need help with time man-agement or work-life balance. The point is, you won't know until you ask.

These types of one-on-one conversations don't occur during normal business hours and standard business operations. They have to be set aside so that you can listen, coach, and mentor. You may not need more than a half-hour per quarter per employee on your team, and some meetings may take only half that amount of time. What can you expect?

- Twenty percent of your team members will step up to these quarterly check-ins with flying colors: resumes will be shared, LinkedIn profiles reviewed together, productivity spreadsheets and achievement calendars discussed, and the like. Challenge your superstars: create an environment in which they can motivate themselves and watch them soar. They will naturally benefit the most from this kind of dedicated one-on-one attention.

- In comparison, 70 percent of your team will undergo the exercise without giving it much thought or prep time. This is the group for you to motivate and incentivize. "Moving the middle" occurs right here, right now. Discuss plans for one to three years and how they want to get there. Ask how they plan to distinguish themselves from their peers. Inquire about their technical skills, education, and additions to their resumes and LinkedIn profiles. Yes, you have to prod and encourage this group more than the 20 percent cohort. But moving even a small percentage of this group to the 20 percent superstar group will surely define you as an outstanding people leader and talent developer. Focus on one employee at a time at this stage: "moving the middle" occurs in drips, not waves, but it's an exercise well worth it.

- Finally, you can expect roughly 10 percent of your employees at any given time to pay scant attention to this quarterly goal-setting and achievement exercise. They will likely not want to participate in their annual review process by preparing a self-review for you in advance. These are the disengaged, the ones who simply want to do their job and be left alone. Should you discipline them for not participating? No. Should you not invite them to quarterly check-in meetings, hold them accountable for creating their IDPs, or avoid meeting with them in advance of their annual performance review to discuss their self-review? No. You still need to meet with these individuals because they're on your team, plain and simple, and you always want to give them a chance to step up. Simply understand that not everyone may be thinking about career or success at any given time and may simply be treading water. What can you do? After you meet with them quarterly, reflect in their annual reviews that they have participated minimally in quarterly reviews, may not have met their goals, or refused to participate in the annual self-evaluation process. That record is real, it's concrete, and it holds them accountable yet creates a narrative of their unwillingness to participate or engage in their work. (Then turn to book 4 of this series—*Leadership Defense*—for help!)

Note: 20-70-10 bell-curve discussions like this aren't literal and won't occur on your particular team at any given time. Such trends can only be seen over much larger data sets, often ten-thousand-plus units/people at a time over long time periods. So, don't look for a true bell curve unless you have a particularly large team! Still, as a rule of thumb, the 20-70-10 bell curve idea places things in perspective by helping you sort out who generally falls into its various categories. This way, you won't accidentally label everyone a superstar (that is, the equivalent of the top 20 percent of the bell curve), which can cause grade inflation during the annual review process when everyone on the team gets the highest score available.

11

THE CRITICAL NATURE OF SELF-EVALUATIONS IN PREPARATION FOR THE ANNUAL REVIEW

The chronological follow-up after three quarterly IDP meetings naturally lies in the annual review. But there's one more important step that shouldn't be overlooked in the performance management / leadership development chain of events: the employee's self-review leading up to the annual performance review meeting. Simply stated, self-review gives employees an opportunity to rate themselves and allows the supervisor to compare those self-ratings with the supervisor's perception of the individual's performance. It gives employees a chance to weigh in on and influence their annual performance review score, which is exactly what you want from a performance management program of any kind.

If you've been managing and measuring employee performance throughout the year, and especially if you've held quarterly coaching check-in sessions, your objective has clearly been to increase your employees' performance, to highlight and recognize their achievements along the way, and to help build their self-confidence in their ability to excel. The annual self-review provides them the opportunity to demonstrate their achievements, show how they've grown, and prepare for their next round of goals over the upcoming review year. It's a logical follow-on to the partnership you've developed, which has so well balanced the company's need to excel with the individual's need to grow, both professionally and personally.

The performance appraisal process is a two-way communication: both employee and supervisor should have input regarding historical performance and future goals. Some companies accomplish this by distributing the performance appraisal form itself to employees and asking them to complete it before the interview. Other organizations encourage employees to provide feedback without necessarily providing any type of feedback mechanism. The model described below represents a healthy compromise: it structures employees' feedback into three main topical areas, allowing individuals the discretion to provide as much or as little detail as they wish.

In general, I don't recommend allowing employees to draft their own performance evaluations on the actual appraisal template. The grading in each performance area and the overall score at the end of the review should be created by the supervisor, not by the staff member. But not asking for employee input before conducting performance appraisals can be disappointing and demotivating for workers because they end up feeling like they have little control over or input into their own career development. In addition, because managers tend to leave out important details that they may have forgotten about but that remain important to the employee, self-reviews should generally be encouraged. They also save the manager lots of time because it falls to the employee to gather and present the data that will make up a significant portion of the appraisal's content.

Therefore, ask your employees to answer the following three groups of questions with as much detail as they prefer to contribute:

Employee Self-evaluation Template

Address your overall performance track record for this review period:

Specifically highlight your achievements that have resulted in increased revenues, decreased expenses, or saved time.

Why is our organization a better place because you worked here this past year?

How have you had to reinvent your job in light of our department's changing needs?

How would you grade yourself in terms of work quality, reliability, production, teamwork, and technical skills?

Comments: _____

_____

_____

_____

In what areas do you need additional support, structure, and direction? Specifically, where can I, as your supervisor, provide you with additional support in terms of acquiring new skills, strengthening your overall performance, or preparing you for your next move in career progression?

Comments: _____

_____

_____

_____

What are your performance goals for the next year? What are the measurable outcomes so that we'll know that you'll have reached those goals?

Comments: _____

_____

_____

_____

These three groups of questions invite your team members to involve themselves in their own career development, make you their coach, and motivate themselves to build "achievement bullets" on their resumes, as well as contemplate next year's self-evaluation exercise.

Not all employees will participate, and some may provide only cursory information. That's okay: the real target audience for this exercise is the top 20 percent of your team who look for ways to build their careers and acquire new skills in tandem with you, their supervisor. Don't be surprised when those super-achievers present you with spreadsheets that describe their career goals, specific skill acquisition, achievement milestones, and the like. But this exercise provides the middle 70 percent of performers an opportunity to distinguish themselves from their peers, hopefully encouraging some to step out of the middle of the pack and join the ranks of the top 20 percent.

Remember, as a leader, you're not responsible for motivating your team members; motivation is internal, and you can't motivate them any more than they can motivate you. As a leader in your organization, however, you *are* responsible for creating an environment in which people can motivate themselves. This self-evaluation exercise achieves that very goal: it gives all your employees—especially your top performers—a chance to involve themselves in their own professional and career development and point out key areas where you can help them. In short, it sets everyone up for success.

SPECIAL NOTE: TRAINING AND THE SELF-EVALUATION

Training opportunities should support individual development plans, which are based on the performance review. Training may include leadership, teambuilding, individual performance, or specific technical skill sets. Feel free to add a fourth element to the self-evaluation template above that invites employees to invest time into researching training opportunities that may motivate them and enhance your team's overall offerings.

Of course, training cannot solve problems caused by misalignment in organizational structure, leadership direction, budgeted resources, or the like. But every employee should have an individual development plan that includes training to help achieve objectives. After all, the glue that binds someone to their company can often be found in the learning curve. And a learning environment makes a more capable, competent, and confident team.

GAINING AGREEMENT ON RATING DEFINITIONS AND OVERALL SCORES BEFORE DRAFTING PERFORMANCE REVIEWS

Before any manager in your organization writes anyone's review, it's important for leaders to discuss with their superiors how to rank-order all staff members. You'll benefit from a tool to help you talk through what can otherwise be very subjective types of considerations.

Let's look at an example. Your company's chief financial officer believes that her team is meeting expectations and performing well, and she intends to award "overall scores" of three to the majority of her staffers, reflecting that they're meeting expectations and performing well. She recognizes that they're a younger team and still have a lot to learn, but their hearts are in the right place, they're dedicated to the organization, and willing to put in long hours. Then she hesitates and thinks, "Then again, my peers in sales and operations will probably award more five scores than anything else, even though their teams are no better than mine. So, maybe I'll need to award fives to everyone in finance as well; otherwise, my group will receive lower merit increases relative to the other departments."

Is it okay if a manager expects everyone on the team to be a five (that is, outstanding, stellar, and able to leap tall buildings in a single bound)? Does it bother you that the head of finance doesn't feel comfortable awarding what she feels is the right score for the majority of her team—three/"meets expectations"—because her peers in other departments will inflate scores for their own teams? How do you get everyone on the same page in terms of distinguishing appropriately between scores and assigning grades that truly reflect the level of performance in that group?

The simple answer lies in communication—discussing perceptions of what the scores actually mean and which employees should be assigned to them. The following rater definition consistency tool can be used as a point of reference for all department heads. The purpose of the tool is to help open the lines of communication and get all leaders "speaking the same language" about what success looks like relative to individual contributions and performance levels over the past year. The definitions are spelled out to paint a clearer picture of just what makes someone exceptional. Individual employees on all leaders' teams can be discussed as a group with grades assigned collectively as a senior leadership team. The tool itself can be broken down as follows:

RATER DEFINITION CONSISTENCY TOOL

Five—Distinguished Performance (≤ 5 percent)

Role model status. Potential successor to immediate supervisor/ highly promotable now. Performed above and beyond under exceptional circumstances during the review period. Generally recognized as number one (top 5 percent) ranking among peer group.

Four—Superior Performance (30 percent)

Overall excellent performer and easy to work with—smart, dedicated, ambitious, and cooperative, but may not yet be ready to promote because there's still more to learn in the current role. May not have been exposed to exceptional circumstances or opportunities that would warrant a higher designation. But definitely an exceptional contributor who exceeds people's expectations in many ways and is a long-term "keeper"—just needs more time in current role to grow and develop and gain additional exposure.

Three—Fully Successful Performance (50 percent)

THREE (A)	THREE (B)
Consistently performs well and is reliable, courteous, and dedicated. Always tries hard and looks for ways of acquiring new skills but doesn't necessarily perform with distinction. Works to live rather than lives to work. May not stand out as a rarity among peers but consistently contributes to the department's efforts and is a valuable member of the team.	Meets expectations overall but may be challenged in particular performance areas. May perform well because of tenure in role and familiarity with workload but does not appear ambitious about learning new things or expanding beyond comfort zone. While performance may be acceptable, conduct may at times be problematic. Tends to resist change or hinder team development.

Two—Partially Successful Performance (10 percent)

Fails to meet minimum performance or conduct expectations in specific areas of responsibility. Is not able to demonstrate consistent improvement. May appear to be burned out or lack motivation and fails to go the extra mile for others. Lacks requisite technical skills or knowledge relating to particular aspects of role. May perform well but conduct is so problematic that the entire year's performance contribution may be invalidated. The performance review may be accompanied by a performance improvement plan (PIP). A partial merit increase or bonus may be awarded.

One—Unsuccessful Performance (≤ 5 percent)

Fails to meet minimum performance or conduct expectations for the role in general. The individual's position is in immediate jeopardy of being lost. The performance review may be accompanied by a performance improvement plan (PIP) or progressive disciplinary documentation stating that failure to demonstrate immediate and sustained improvement will result in dismissal. No merit increase or bonus should be awarded.

The percentages next to each scoring category reflect what you'd normally expect to see if your company's scoring results fell under a typical bell-curve configuration. Also, notice that the "three" category—meets expectations / fully successful performance—has two subsets: one for those who really try hard but don't necessarily perform with distinction and another for those who perform satisfactorily but don't necessarily give it their best effort. Distinguishing between a three (a) and a three (b) can be particularly helpful when engaging in dialogues and discussions regarding individual contribution levels.

How these general parameters fit your organization and what they might look like at any given time should indeed differ from year to year. What makes most sense is to discuss your perceptions as a senior team and then one-on-one with your boss before drafting or issuing performance reviews. Start with the highest generally recognized performers first and see if you can agree on why the fives are fives. Your discussion can then proceed to fours, threes, twos, and ones. The point is, get the conversation going. From senior leaders to frontline supervisors, conversations like these need to happen to raise awareness of your organizational expectations and to provide leaders with benchmarks and guideposts to align their assessments. And this, more than anything, eliminates or significantly reduces the tendency toward grade inflation, where managers score employees higher than they should for fear of confrontation.

What's the difference between a four and a five? Is it simply a matter of someone who's able to promote into the boss's role now as opposed to two years from now? Is the difference attributable to outstanding circumstances that year that allowed the individual to assume responsibilities well beyond their job description? Likewise, what's the difference between a three (b) and a two? Is it acceptable to have someone on the team who's technically capable due to long tenure in the role but who appears to demonstrate little ambition or interest in anything outside of their immediate area? What about occasional inappropriate conduct—how "occasional" does it have to be to fail someone for the entire review year? Should we award partial merit increases to anyone who receives an overall score of two, or should we take that money and return it to the pool to reward the higher performers?

As you could surmise, there aren't necessarily right or wrong answers to these questions, and much of this is subject to debate. But it's healthy debate, and it's wise to have at least one discussion like this before committing your energy to drafting annual reviews. Otherwise, you'll end up with an entire management team working in a silo and "self-interpreting" what the organization wants to see in terms of proposed overall performance review scores without any guidelines or structure. This is how successful organizations fine-tune performance over time in a performance-driven company.

13

THE ANNUAL REVIEW MEETING
OBJECTIVE FEEDBACK PLUS RENEWED ENGAGEMENT

No matter how much preparation goes into an employee's self-evaluation, and no matter how well the quarterly coaching and IDP reviews have gone throughout the year, the face-to-face annual review tends to be the most stressful work conversation that employees will hear all year. Ditto for the managers who deliver them because of the potential confrontational nature of the exercise. At its core, there is a fundamental, underlying sense that judgment is about to be rendered—both objective and subjective, observational and (unfortunately) judgmental. Deep down, it makes people feel ill at ease. After all, no one wants to be judged, especially with the tremendous amount of feedback about to be shared. Many people worry, "Will I be blindsided by anything I didn't see? Have I been reading the tea leaves correctly all year long in terms of how my boss views my contributions? Will my overall score garner the highest percentage merit increase? Will my performance warrant a bonus?"

And don't forget the manager's side of the equation: "Will I be blindsiding her with any of the feedback I'm about to share?

How honest can I be about *X*, which she's really not quite getting? We work together side by side every day: Will our relationship survive candid feedback, or am I about to get myself into a cold war? And what if the feedback is so disappointing that she decides to look for another job elsewhere?"

Fear not: there are ways to make this whole process less nerve-racking. The self-review helps tremendously because you know where the employee is coming from—you'll have had an opportunity to look behind the curtain and learn about their personal ambitions, so you're off to a good start. The quarterly IDP coaching meetings (if the employee kept up with them) gave you opportunities to touch base throughout the year, so there shouldn't be many surprises. Finally, even if there's new negative feedback to share, there are options for doing so in a caring and empathetic way that will help the individual assume responsibility and accountability for continuing to strengthen those areas.

One option is to share the document with the employee and read it aloud. The tone of your voice adds a human touch that tones down the harshness of the black-and-white words on paper. Another alternative is to share the document with the employee about an hour before the meeting so she can read it on her own time privately and come to terms with any emotional responses it may trigger. This gives her a chance to think about it and prepare for the meeting rather than hear about things for the first time in front of you. Either approach can work, depending on your communication style and relationship with your staff members.

Next, in terms of your approach, share compliments early in the dialogue to recognize the individual's contributions and set her mind at ease. Then continue with the "feedback sandwich" approach through the rest of the meeting: compliments, then constructive feedback and criticism, then encouragement. Discussing deficiencies during the criticism stage is always difficult, but in fairness, most people are good to great performers, so the review shouldn't overly weigh on deficiencies unless the individual clearly isn't meeting minimal performance expectations. Focus the majority of the review, instead, on achievements and building on the individual's strengths.

The dialogue opener invites the employee to "judge" her own performance, and it's a healthy opener to the exercise. First, whether she received the review an hour before the meeting or she's receiving it now for the first time, it puts her in charge of providing an objective overall assessment of her performance and contributions throughout the year. Contrary to what you might think, most employees tend to be harder on themselves than you would otherwise be. That places you in the role of coach and mentor to lift them up, so to speak, rather than render judgment and be perceived as "putting them down" right from the outset.

Next, discuss your point of view relative to the employee's initial feedback. Read through the review with your employee, explaining briefly how you evaluated her in each section. Once the read-through is complete, allow the employee a few moments to share her initial feedback. Answer any questions about the categories contained within the review that require further detail or discussion, including the goal section. Field questions relating to the overall score.

Of course, there may be disagreement along the way. And sometimes—although rarely—employees see themselves as outstanding, high performers, when in reality they're struggling to meet the minimum performance requirements of their job or otherwise failing their annual review. But those topics deserve deeper-dive considerations (which I've covered more in book 4—*Leadership Defense*—of *The Paul Falcone Workplace Leadership Series*). For now, simply appreciate the rhythm of the cycle: Setting goals helps keep people aligned, focused, and on point. Quarterly coaching meetings where you discuss employees' progress toward their individual development plans emphasize their professional and career development, while you get the opportunity to help them course correct or pivot, depending on what's going on at the time. The self-evaluation then gives them a level of control as well as skin in the game in terms of assessing themselves and having input into their formal annual review. And a new set of stretch goals are then established to help them become stronger players in their own right and prepare for their next move in career progression, if they so choose.

Always try to keep performance management this simple. Always remind your team members that you support their personal, professional, and career growth. They can't hear that message enough. Involving them in the process at all stages shows respect. Engaging with them in constructive feedback—if couched appropriately—helps them become more self-aware and (ideally) willing to change. It's a healthy cycle in which the employee does the majority of the work: You, the manager, simply create the space for this to happen. Space on your calendar, for sure, but even more important, space for your employees to grow and explore, to stretch and safely fail. That's what career coaching is all about, and it, above all else, should become your leadership brand and mantra going forward in your own career.

HINT:
GREAT LEADERSHIP STEMS FROM
HIGH EMPATHY AND HIGH ACCOUNTABILITY

From a career development standpoint for your employees, make empathy and accountability key talking points throughout the year. Even if these two traits are not specifically called out in your company's performance review template, consider making them critical performance factors that you address in the "narrative comments" section of the performance review.

- Leaders who demonstrate high levels of empathy and accountability often garner greater loyalty from their subordinates and peers who feel understood and supported (empathy) while being challenged to do their best work every day (accountability).
- Likewise, leaders who are able to combine these two core traits typically ensure harmonious relationships among team members, increasing both individual and group confidence and productivity.

Leaders with high empathy and accountability often foster a culture that centers around relationships and having one another's backs. Such leadership traits often result in high productivity, lower turnover, and confidence in a shared vision. Whether you lead managers or individual contributors, talk about this golden combination of high empathy and high accountability with your team members and discuss what it might look like in day-to-day operations and how it can be strengthened and encouraged going forward.

14

PERFORMANCE REVIEW DOCUMENTATION TIPS
STRENGTHENING YOUR WRITTEN MESSAGE

It would be wise to dedicate time to strengthening your performance appraisal documentation skills. How you document is a critical element of the performance review process, and a few healthy reminders can go a long way in terms of enhancing your message while also protecting the company from unwanted legal scrutiny. Following are tips that you can apply fairly easily and that will strengthen your message.

First, be sure to avoid writing anything that could be interpreted as discriminatory. You may not document or reference anything protected by privacy or employee protection laws. For example, writing "Michael, you are performing well since you began your new medication to combat depression, and I encourage you to continue" could very well violate the protections afforded by the Americans with Disabilities Act if the individual is later denied a promotion or terminated for cause. Similarly, if you reference an individual's age, ethnicity, sexual or gender orientation, religious beliefs, medical history, or any other categories protected under Title VII of the Civil Rights Act or other state worker protection laws, then your own documentation could be used against your company in a court of law.

Further, if an employee was on a leave of absence for a significant part of the review period, simply document that "Michael was on an approved leave of absence from May 10 to August 8" and leave it at that. The reason for the leave (pregnancy, workers' comp injury, stress leave) is superfluous and should not be included as part of the formal record that the performance review establishes. It follows that all performance appraisals should be reviewed in advance by your human resources or legal departments before they are shared with your employees to ensure, among other things, that no discriminatory language exists.

Second, avoid the term *attitude* in your formal business communication with your subordinates. "Attitude" is a very subjective judgment that courts typically dismiss because it is often associated with a mere difference of opinion or a personality conflict. Instead, be sure to describe the objective behaviors that create a negative perception of the employee in others' eyes. Only behaviors and actions that can be observed and documented belong in workplace discussions and may be presented as evidence in court. For example, replace an admonition like this:

As we have discussed throughout the year, you have received many complaints regarding your *attitude*. You need to demonstrate immediate improvement in this area.

with something concrete like this:

Peggy received a written warning on January 14 for raising her voice in anger and using profane language directed at a coworker.

The disciplinary warning specifically stated that if she ever again lost control of her temper, used profane language in the workplace, or demonstrated behavior or conduct that could be perceived as hostile or threatening, further disciplinary action up to and including termination could result.

Third, use the phrase "for example" at least two or three times in an individual performance appraisal. Managers often make sweeping comments about perceptions without documenting the factual circumstances that justify their point—for example:

Your customer care skills are satisfactory, but you sometimes require additional assistance in this area.

That's not specific enough. Instead, write something more concrete and instructional for the employee by including an example like this:

For example, on June 14 of this year, we discussed vendor A's situation where an April 1 invoice fell through the cracks and wasn't discovered until May 30. When you discovered the variance, you didn't reach out to the client to acknowledge it and instead waited an additional two weeks for me to return from vacation before escalating the matter. As I shared with you at the time, I would have expected you to contact the client immediately, apologize for the error on our part, and reach out directly to our accounts payable department to rectify the situation and pay the vendor.

Fourth, use the terminology "needs improvement" cautiously in your narrative writing, as it may not convey the message you intend. Stating that performance or behavior "needs improvement" is not the same as stating that it doesn't meet company standards or is unsatisfactory. Similarly, documenting that "Richard has been *spoken to* regarding excessive absenteeism and tardiness" does not convey that his performance was unacceptable. Don't assume that the employee understood (or a jury would agree) that just because you *spoke about* performance that *needed improvement*, it was assumed to be substandard. Again, you'll need to be more specific by stating, for example, that the performance or behavior "fails to meet acceptable standards" or "does not currently meet company expectations."

Fifth, document the efforts you've made to help the employee meet performance standards throughout the review period. When writing annual performance appraisals, for example, include the fact that you gave the employee a copy of the attendance policy, paid for her to attend a workshop on dealing with interpersonal conflict in the workplace, or encouraged her to take an accounting course at a local college. Likewise, congratulate the individual for using the company's tuition reimbursement program to complete an online certification or licensing program. Such documentation will serve as evidence that your organization acted responsibly as a good corporate citizen by investing in the employee or by attempting to proactively rehabilitate someone facing particular difficulties during the review year.

Finally, when structuring future goals and development plans on paper, follow the "I expect you to . . . by . . ." format. For example, don't simply write this:

> In the upcoming review period, you must improve your client relations skills and better utilize your time.

Instead, strengthen that statement by applying the "I expect you to . . . by . . ." format:

I expect you to improve your client relations skills *by* following up with customers within two hours of their initial calls, *by* meeting them in their offices rather than asking them to come to yours, and *by* maintaining weekly contact regarding the status of their work order processing.

This structure will help you clearly outline your performance expectations and how they will be concretely measured. Clarity in your written message will not only protect your company from potential outside legal challenges; it will help build a shared sense of open communication, a greater sense of partnership, and increased accountability with your workers.

15

ADDRESSING TODAY'S CRITICAL COMPETENCIES

INNOVATION, REMOTE WORK, AND CHANGE AND AGILITY

B ecause work continues to change and evolve at such a rapid pace, managers need to develop employees who are adept at change, willing to bend, and capable of taking smart risks. New skills, competencies, and attitudes are required to navigate today's changing workplace priorities. It's critical that you capture and incorporate the drivers of organizational success into your performance appraisal template—the "annual report" that captures the "evolutionary change at revolutionary speed" mindset of today's business world. Your company's performance review template should be revised every few years, not passed down from generation to generation as a static document. While you may not be in human resources to make this happen, recommending it from an operational leadership standpoint is highly recommended.

You can either amend the entire template or simply add a module to the existing template. Whatever the case, it's important that you communicate the values and priorities that you hold dear to your team in addition to the core competencies outlined in your organization's performance review template. Of course, check with your senior management team before going down this path, but as long as your expectations are clear, you should generally have the discretion to highlight certain traits or augment certain areas on the appraisal form or as part of the appraisal process itself.

Agility, flexibility, adaptability, and remote work are all excellent places to start. With these hotter demands in focus, help your team understand what success looks like by sharing descriptors of successful performance. Identify first the core drivers that you want to highlight, then focus on building out descriptors that raise the bar and help workers focus on meeting new, heightened expectations. Following are some sample competencies and descriptors for each of these areas.

Adaptability and Flexibility

- Identifies unique ways of creating value and encourages others to employ their curiosity and imagination.
- Demonstrates the ability to multitask and handle pressure or crisis situations. Adjusts priorities to meet team or organizational needs.
- Remains resolute and calm when faced with challenges or seemingly inadequate resources.
- Encourages team members to take appropriate risks and embrace change.
- Regularly combines natural curiosity and gut intuition with sound analysis and reasoning to strengthen our "organizational forecasting ability."
- Readily develops strategies to reflect our changing business priorities.
- Effectively translates strategies into objectives and action plans.

Creativity and Innovation

- ■ Turns ideas into action, puts creativity to work, and develops strategies for innovation.
- ■ Rethinks routine processes and finds unique solutions for adding customer value.
- ■ Funnels creative recommendations into practical applications.
- ■ Employs right-brain imagination, creativity, and intuition with left-brain logic and planning.
- ■ Searches constantly for new innovation methods, techniques, and tools.
- ■ Regularly encourages greater collaboration and open discussion with peers and team members to foster a culture of innovation.
- ■ Participates in and/or leads diverse product teams to cultivate a broader range of perspectives, knowledge, thought, and creativity.

Change-Management and Versatility

- ■ Willingly embraces last-minute changes in direction and unexpected changes in plans.
- ■ Creates a friendly and inclusive work environment when faced with changes in direction or deadlines.
- ■ Demonstrates the ability to multitask and handle pressure or crisis situations. Adjusts priorities to meet team and organizational needs.
- ■ Communicates with management appropriately when faced with changing priorities or the need to pivot away from a preplanned course of action.
- ■ Remains resolute and calm when faced with challenges or seemingly inadequate resources.

- Helps team members embrace change and adapt to a "new normal" when faced with unforeseen challenges.
- Constantly looks for ways of using new technologies to increase efficiency.

Remote Work

- Displays the appropriate amount of self-discipline, organizational habits, and written and verbal communication skills to produce consistently and predictably.
- Possesses strong collaborative and teambuilding skills to foster group productivity and create a friendly and inclusive work environment.
- Demonstrates high levels of self-motivation, knowing what needs to be done, and creative problem-solving and flexibility to find necessary solutions.
- Remains prepared to adapt to new ways of working, sporadic changes, and unexpected situations, including technical challenges arising from internet and Wi-Fi issues, server problems, and logins.
- Manages time effectively and remains accountable for all deliverables, without the need for constant check-ins from management.
- Exercises strong independent work habits, continuously learning from changes in direction, and makes good use of project management software, shared documents and folders, and dedicated internal channels to communicate fluidly with team members.
- Finds efficient ways to complete projects, knowing who to ask when stuck or in need of direction.

With these enhanced descriptors and competencies mapped out, you can then discuss how to achieve a particular score in that area (for example, what a score of three, four, or five might look like in real life). It's a fun exercise that typically goes beyond the performance review template that your organization employs for annual reviews. It likewise gives you the opportunity to share what you feel is important for your department or team and describes how you intend to capture this feedback in the review itself (for example, in a separate narrative section under "Comments"). You just might find that when you share ideas for highlighting the "hottest skills" in demand today that may not be captured on your existing performance review template, senior management will not only support your initiative, but they may adopt your practices for other parts of the organization or agree to amend the performance appraisal template itself.

16

WHEN YOUR PERFORMANCE APPRAISAL TEMPLATE DOESN'T QUITE GET YOU WHERE YOU WANT TO GO

One particular challenge that you should be prepared to face at performance review time is this: many organizations match annual performance reviews to employee job descriptions, and that's a mistake because job descriptions often define performance with the lowest acceptable standards. Performance reviews, instead, should aim for the highest level of performance in their competency descriptors.

For example, here's how the challenge plays itself out in real life with a traditional performance review descriptor for a customer service representative:

The Job Description Competency:
- Provides prompt, courteous, and professional customer communication.
- Provides timely and well-informed advice to customers.
- Demonstrates sufficient knowledge of company products and cross-selling skills to ensure a high level of customer satisfaction.
- Prioritizes workload based on customers' needs.

- Regularly adheres to scripts and selling tips.
- Skillfully overcomes customer objections.
- Consistently gains necessary authorizations and approvals for one-off exceptions to policy.

Ho-hum. With such a low level of performance expectations, it becomes easy for managers to award scores of four and five (that is, exceeds expectations or distinguished performance). Likewise, workers can become resentful for receiving a score of three—"meets expectations," which they equate as "average"— when the bar is set so low. Now look at the heightened performance review description below as a point of comparison:

The Performance Review Competency:
- Exhibits role model behavior in terms of demonstrating total commitment to outstanding customer service. Provides knock-your-socks-off service that consistently exceeds client expectations. Consistently exhibits creativity and flexibility in resolving customer issues.
- Remains customer-oriented, flexible, and responsive to last-minute changes in plans. Regularly puts the human relationship above the transaction. Looks always to surprise customers with unanticipated benefits, including lower costs and shortened delivery time frames.
- Effectively exceeds customer expectations by providing timely feedback and follow-up in an empathetic and caring way. Tactfully informs customers when their requests cannot be met and escalates matters for further review and approval as appropriate.
- Takes pride in building relationships with even the most challenging clients. Enjoys identifying "out-of-the-box"

solutions for clients with special needs. Goes beyond
customer satisfaction by driving customer loyalty, as
evidenced by a high rate of repeat business.

These enhanced descriptors drive higher performance expectations, set the bar at a new level, and reflect performance relative
to a much higher standard. If employees can honestly meet these
heightened expectations, then they deserve a higher score of four
or five. Many will realize, however, that a score of three is more
suitable relative to the heightened expectations outlined above.
In short, the performance review competency reveals the true
level of exceptional or distinguished performance, removing the
false expectation from the employee's mind that merely meeting
the terms outlined on the job description warrants a higher performance review score.

Don't worry if you feel your performance review template
isn't keeping up with the times. Your dedicated focus to these
critical areas will go a long way in improving your employees'
focus on achievements and accomplishments. You'll also be helping them build the most critical competencies for the greater
work marketplace, keeping their skills and marketability up to
par and relevant. The only step left is to help them incorporate
these heightened achievements into their self-evaluations, resumes, and LinkedIn profiles.

A job description lists basic competencies required to perform a job. The annual performance review, in comparison,
should set the bar progressively higher over time. It should reflect excellence so that employees can gauge their performance
and conduct relative to the highest, not most minimal, standards
and expectations. Raising expectations in your core competency
categories drives higher levels of performance. It also makes it

easier to avoid grade inflation, a cardinal sin in most organizations, when supervisors score employees higher than they actually deserve.

Change is the new normal. Let your performance review drive the key goals and outcomes you're looking to foster throughout your organization. And if it doesn't because it's older and hasn't been updated in a while, share your performance philosophy with your team and explain why your beliefs and strategies will help them remain marketable and current relative to today's biggest challenges. Your performance review exercises will take on a whole new meaning and level of significance in light of the demands you're facing and the strides you're making in today's challenging and ever-changing business environment.

17

CREATING AN EFFECTIVE
PERFORMANCE IMPROVEMENT PLAN

While this book focuses on leadership offense and motivation, it's critical to address performance improvement plans in this chapter because they're tied so directly to annual performance reviews. The term "performance improvement plan," or PIP, has different meanings in different workplaces:

- In the most traditional sense, a PIP is used in conjunction with a failed annual performance review and serves as an action plan to turn around individual performance or conduct and return employee performance to an acceptable level.

- Likewise, employers often use the term PIP in progressive disciplinary documentation to outline performance expectations, define resources available, and invite the employee's feedback and participation in the turnaround.

- Still other organizations use PIP as synonymous with a written warning of some sort. "Putting someone on a PIP" is another way of saying "writing them up."

In our case, we'll stick with the traditional usage—that is, a performance action plan following a failed annual review. PIPs typically consist of five common elements that:

1. identify specific areas of improvement (related to either performance or conduct);
2. provide concrete examples of the problematic behavior or performance issue;
3. outline expectations for meeting and/or exceeding the terms of the PIP;
4. identify training and support along with scheduled touch points (progress meetings); and
5. are time-bound, typically lasting from 60 to 120 days, with the average at 90 days.

Note, however, that PIPs aren't necessarily considered part of the organization's progressive discipline program. Generally speaking, they are an action plan for the employee and supervisor to work together to address significant concerns regarding the employee's performance or conduct. Many employees fear "being placed on a PIP" because it could be viewed as a first step toward termination. That may indeed eventually be the case if the individual isn't able to meet the terms outlined in the PIP. PIPs are serious; unless the employee is able to demonstrate significant and sustained improvement, PIPs will serve to move the written record in a new direction, pointing to the individual's inability or unwillingness to meet expectations for the role. Progressive discipline or a termination for cause may indeed follow.

If a company opts to include a PIP as part of its progressive disciplinary program, the PIP will likely serve as the equivalent of a verbal warning. Assuming the employee hasn't been disciplined before, the failed review triggers a PIP; if the terms of the PIP aren't met, the company may then issue a written warning (that is, skipping the first step in the formal progressive disciplinary paradigm of a documented verbal warning). Likewise, if the PIP was issued for behavioral or conduct-related reasons (for example, insubordination, bullying, or retaliation), the PIP may serve as a written warning. Failure to meet its terms could result in a final written warning. Finally, if the employee is already on a final written warning at the time of the annual review and then fails the annual review, the PIP could serve as notice that failure to meet its terms will result in immediate dismissal (thereby serving as a formal notice that his position is now in immediate jeopardy of being lost).

As you can guess, much depends on the nature of the issue, the employee's tenure, and the disciplinary record already in place. Speak with qualified legal counsel about the appropriate use of the PIP in cases when the PIP will be used as a disciplinary measure or when serious conduct infractions may be involved, as each case will depend on the facts in place at the time.

Next, it's critically important to address failed performance in a PIP because no employee should receive two failed performance reviews in a row. A failed performance review negates an entire year of contributions. It's serious and significant. Therefore, a failed review should trigger an immediate management response to engage the problematic issues and turn the situation around. Failure to do so on management's part is a big miss. If an employee fails back-to-back performance reviews (or three or more in a row), it actually makes it harder to terminate the person. After all, a court may reason, you've tolerated the problem all these years: Why are you arbitrarily moving to termination now?

Hint: when you determine it's getting close to termination, be sure to issue progressive disciplinary warnings in addition to the PIP and the annual performance review so you have a clearer record that you've accorded due process and the worker understands that his position is now in immediate jeopardy. The back-to-back failed reviews won't necessarily make the employee fear his job is at risk if you've tolerated the problems for years and never did anything about it. The final written warning, for example, might read:

> This is your last chance, and you are now in immediate jeopardy
> of losing your position. Failure to demonstrate immediate and
> sustained improvement will result in termination.

(More on this in book 4—*Leadership Defense*.)

Note that you don't need a particular form or template to create a PIP; a narrative summary that includes the points above will suffice. If you prefer a template, however, apply something simple like this:

PERFORMANCE IMPROVEMENT PLAN	
Description of Underperformance	
Aim of the Performance Improvement Plan	
Plan Start Date	
Plan End Date	

Objective	Success Criteria	Additional Support Required	Review Schedule	Objective Outcome

X _____

Employee Signature   Date

X _____

Supervisor Signature   Date

PART
3

ON MOTIVATION AND PROFESSIONAL AND CAREER DEVELOPMENT

Rewarding people for achievement is far preferable to punishing them for failure. Building on people's strengths always begets a higher return than shoring up their weaknesses. Allowing people to assume greater responsibilities is better for them and for the organization because no one knows the work or the customers better than those on the front line. Creating an environment marked by innovation, creativity, and imagination can only come from an enlightened workforce with the right incentives and recognition programs in place.

How do you motivate workers through tough times? How do you create a more welcoming and inclusive work environment? And how do you change your organization's culture? The answer: one day and one step at a time. Make no mistake, however: it all begins with you.

No single manager can turn villains into heroes or otherwise wave a magic wand and reinvent a company's culture. But you're the first domino. You can make an impact in your unit, department, or division tomorrow that can alter your team's output and trajectory. You can find new ways of motivating your top producers and making work fun again by simply changing your underlying thought about who you are and who you choose to be. It all stems from the respect, recognition, and trust that you sense and share with your team members every day.

Other books in this series have addressed how to make many of these things happen. This chapter focuses on creating a healthy work environment where team members can find new ways of motivating and reinventing themselves in light of the newest challenges coming your way. Remember these words of Napoleon Hill:

You can succeed best and quickest by helping others to succeed.

Nothing ensures success like ensuring another's success. And there is someone who is looking for your help and your support today. Lift that person up, give that person credit, and do whatever you can to help that person succeed. Such are the lessons of servant leadership. And such are the makings of great leaders. And always remember: what goes around, comes around.

18

MOTIVATING STAFF WITHOUT MONEY
THE HOLY GRAIL OF WORKPLACE ENGAGEMENT

They say there are two kinds of employees who quit companies: those who quit and leave versus those who quit and *stay*. We've all experienced working with and leading employees who wish they were anywhere other than at your company—it shows in all aspects of what they do, and their dissatisfaction (or at least apathy) seeps from their pores. It will always be your toughest job as a leader to turn around people who have long lost the motivation to make a difference and a positive contribution to the team.

Let's start with one basic assumption: the weight of the world is not on your shoulders to keep people happy, especially in light of the challenges, change, and churn that so many workers are experiencing in light of corporate America's shifting priorities. Few companies have had opportunities to promote people internally; many have withheld bonuses and even annual merit pool increases because the bottom line has been squeezed so tightly. More important, there exists an underlying tension that corporate America is about to burst—once the market frees itself up, employees will scatter to the winds in hope of making up for lost time career-wise.

Therefore, now is the time to look at the latter half of the "recruitment and *retention*" equation. Retention programs and incentives tend to go by the wayside when the market is flat, and no one has anywhere to go. For retention programs to be effective, however, they need to be in place for a year or so for employees to have time to buy into the program and receive its benefits. Therefore, the time to begin recognizing, appreciating, and motivating your staff is now. That doesn't mean you have to bring your corporate pom-poms to work and play cheerleader. There are a few relatively simple ways that could help you create an environment in which people could motivate themselves.

INCREASE COMPETITION AMONG YOUR COMPANY AND YOUR COMPETITORS

More companies adhere to the philosophy of minimal communication rather than "open-book" management. In other words, senior executives often assume that the less their employees know, the better. "I want them to come in and do their work, not busy themselves learning about our organization's P&L statement" goes the old-fashioned logic. Even if your senior management team adheres to this closed-communication style, practice open-book management with your own staff. Whenever possible, research your organization on social media sites like Glassdoor.com to find out what's documented about your culture and work style. Other websites to spur employee research include:

- Google News: news.google.com.
- LinkedIn, Facebook, Instagram, and Twitter company pages.

▓ D&B Hoovers' commercial database provides both free and subscription-based services covering public and private as well as domestic and international companies: https://www.dnb.com/business-directory.html).

▓ Guidestar.org and CharityNavigator.org focus on nonprofits.

▓ CorporateInformation.com offers free and subscription-based information on international companies: https://www.corporateinformation.com/Company-Advanced-Search.aspx.

▓ PrivCo provides access to general business information about private companies for free; subscription services are also available: https://www.privco.com.

▓ Open Corporates is the world's largest free database of company records: https://opencorporates.com.

▓ BizStats is a website dedicated to providing industry (rather than company) information: http://www.bizstats.com/net-profit-risk.

There are many other company research websites, of course, but get your people digging into your company, its history, its competitors, and industry trends, and you can likely garner a healthy sense of competition and curiosity to reengage some who may take your organization for granted or otherwise have forgotten its uniqueness.

Likewise, assign a small team to review the Bureau of Labor Statistics' *Occupational Outlook Handbook* (www.bls.gov/ooh) to investigate specific roles and career paths found in your department and their ten-year projections in terms of job growth. For example, if the general economy will grow jobs at 4 percent per year over the next ten years and human resource positions are growing at 7 percent, that's nice to know. But the spreadsheet on the site is an incredible eye-opener: HR jobs in publishing will be down 14 percent but in digital publishing up 23 percent. HR jobs in health care and the sciences will be up 55 percent but at the post office will be down 38 percent. In essence, you'll develop your own "corporate futurists" who can research trends and patterns in your industry or sector and have a chance to better understand their career paths and industry potential. Little does more to stimulate interest and competition than pointing employees to the right tools where they can educate themselves (and the rest of your staff). Knowledge is power, and free online resources provide invaluable information about your industry, company, and job growth.

START A BOOK-OF-THE-QUARTER CLUB

You've heard of the Book-of-the-Month Club? Well, that schedule may be a little too aggressive for your team, but if you're looking to stimulate your staff and challenge them to look outside the box, then this "best practice" may win some big fans for you. Simply decide on one book that you'd all like to complete within, say, sixty or ninety days. Assign each member of your staff a chapter to present on, and have that individual discuss the merits of the chapter in your weekly staff meetings. The real challenge will lie in getting your employees to apply the theoretical knowledge from the book to the day-to-day workplace. The company should pay for the books, but a few hundred dollars per year will never be as well spent or have such a potential return on investment.

INJECT INTERMITTENT ROTATIONAL ASSIGNMENTS

Some Fortune 500 organizations have very formal job-rotation programs that may last several years and transect the globe. Assignments require relocation and may benefit from foreign language acquisition or a healthy knowledge of immigration law (think visas, green cards, work permits, and the like). While those grandiose programs no doubt add incredible value to the overall employment experience and the individual's long-term value to the company, most organizations will certainly have to go smaller in terms of their ideals and goals for exposing key employees to other areas of the business to increase their awareness and knowledge.

But don't let the smaller nature of the project scale fool you: staff rotations on an occasional, limited basis allow employees to learn new skills and develop new perspectives on their work. Intermittent rotational assignments could begin with half-day jaunts into other departments' operations, sitting side by side to listen in on calls, or accompanying field employees to customers' residences or places of business. Rotations help people broaden their knowledge about their own career interests as well and gain a comprehensive perspective of the organization's operations. Having an insurance adjuster sit in with an underwriter, a budget analyst sit in with an international finance person, or a recruiter spend a half-day with an employee relations specialist can be an excellent way to help people broaden their outlook and gain exposure to parts of the business they can otherwise only guess about.

In fact, there are myriad ways to motivate staff without money. Don't let budget hold you back: look for free online resources, point your employees in the right direction, and help them learn how to dissect a company, an industry, or their own career trajectories. While nothing may appear to be as effective as cash, those free resources online can go a long way in stimulating interest, reengaging people, and helping them develop research skills that they can use for the rest of their careers.

19

THE NATURE OF MOTIVATION

FIVE STEPS FOR QUICK TURNAROUNDS

When you ask people why they work, a common response might be, "Because I have to," or "Because of the money." And while that may be a true and sincere answer in many ways, it speaks to people who hold "jobs" rather than build careers. Depending on your line of work, that may be okay. But chances are, if you're holding this book right now in the palm of your hand and reading it cover to cover, you're likely dealing with employees looking to build careers and stand out among their peers. As the saying goes, "If you love what you do, you'll never have to work a day again in your life." Although that may sound a bit too altruistic for most of us, it speaks to a kernel of truth: at its core, work is meant to fulfill us, engage us, and provide a certain amount of psychic income that goes beyond paychecks and bonuses. It gives us an opportunity to define who we are, to be part of a greater whole, and to make a true difference by what we contribute.

For most of us, even a moderate amount of self-examination and career introspection will reveal that we want to make a positive difference; we want to learn, grow, and develop new skills;

and we want to help others develop according to their talents so they can feel fulfilled and experience satisfaction in defining who they are and what they want to be. To truly understand the nature of motivation and how to create the right kind of workplace that allows others to gain traction and define themselves, you've got to look at your own fundamental assumptions about human behavior.

For example, if you believe that work can be a win-win-win for employee, manager, and company, then creating an engaged workforce should remain a noble goal. Likewise, if you feel that people will exercise self-direction and self-control in the service of projects and goals they've committed to, then you must realize that the key factor in motivation lies in setting up people for success and then simply getting out of the way—taking a "less is more" approach to management and clearing the way for them to find their own creative solutions to the problems at hand. Further, the "average bear" worker looks to assume responsibility, share recognition, and exercise a high degree of imagination, innovation, and creativity in the solution of organizational challenges large and small. Yes, if you believe all these things, then you're simply looking for a way to funnel people's energies to experience more success for themselves and others.

Since the time scientists seriously began studying the nature of work in the nineteenth century, there's been a constant back-and-forth between two competing schools of thought:

1. Workers naturally shun work, do as little as they can get away with without being disciplined, and must be closely watched and guarded, lest they take advantage of the company and hasten its demise with little regard to others who run it or otherwise make their living there.

2. Leadership's responsibility is to create conditions that make people want to offer maximum discretionary effort, help others succeed, and excel by standing out among their peers.

You know the end to this particular story: encouraging workers to find their own individualized solutions to workplace challenges and identifying new ways of inventing themselves in light of their organization's changing needs is far preferable to imposing a system of controls and mandates that needs to be forced on workers who either don't understand or care to learn more about the company's objectives or how they fit into the broader solution in their own unique way.

PRAISE AND RECOGNIZE HARD WORK

By far, the most dramatic and immediate change in your organizational culture will stem from your willingness and ability to praise employees and recognize their achievements. Recognition need not be monetary. In fact, many consulting firms that specialize in reward-and-recognition programs will tell you that research shows that public praise and recognition scores higher in workers' minds than a cash card or check in a sealed envelope. There are plenty of simple and effective ways for leaders to recognize employees. Sometimes it's as simple as a handwritten thank-you note. Encourage your team members to follow your lead in recognizing others for a job well done. There are multiple apps available that focus on highlighting employee achievements and sharing good news. Consider purchasing one, especially if your team works remotely and connects more easily via electronic media. Praise and acknowledge good work openly, catch people being good, and consider organizing recognition events to honor bigger accomplishments, especially those reached by a team working closely together.

HELP EMPLOYEES FULFILL THEIR CAREER GOALS

Career development is a key driver of employee satisfaction. Your strongest performers will always be resume builders. Providing opportunities for talented individuals to do their best work every day, combined with training and educational opportunities, will go a long way in helping people achieve their career advancement goals. Become an organization known for having a commitment to professional development. Provide networking opportunities for your staffers to meet leaders from other parts of the organization over team lunch meetings. Serve as a mentor and coach to your direct reports by asking them about their longer-term goals and how you could help them get there. Show that you're interested in the whole person, not just the one who shows up at work. You'll likely find that people will respond in kind to the heightened dose of positive attention and enthusiasm they're garnering.

MOVE DISSATISFIED EMPLOYEES OUT OF THE ORGANIZATION

We all know the story of the worm in the apple. Some workers are simply unhappy souls. They'll look for reasons to prove you wrong or otherwise act out "on principle" about any potential shortcomings that they identify within the organization. These people tend to suffer from "victim's syndrome" or some type of entitlement mentality that kills camaraderie and teamwork. Whatever they touch and whatever they're up to typically results in a net negative for themselves, their peers, and the organization as a whole.

While it's admittedly easier said than done, removing these unhappy players from the workplace will often spike engagement and enthusiasm immediately, as coworkers experience an immediate sense of relief since they no longer have to walk on eggshells around that person. Removing obstacles is key to developing a motivated team, and sometimes those obstacles wear pants and dresses and report to the office every morning at eight thirty. Simply put, you can't motivate everyone all the time: life isn't that easy. When you've identified someone who refuses to be happy, to get along with others, or who otherwise looks to share misery despite your best efforts to look for the best in people, find a way to remove them respectfully but lawfully (as these individuals will often be the first to sue). Reason to yourself that 3–5 percent of your workforce will fall under this category at any given time throughout your career, so work closely with human resources and your immediate supervisor to "help them be successful elsewhere."

PLUG LEAKS

If you look at most employee opinion survey categories, you'll see that "Employee Relationships with Management" and "Working Environment" are typically two of the top five categories. Respectful treatment of all employees at all levels, trust, open communication, and the relationship with the immediate supervisor will typically cover the majority of questions found on a typical survey. Why? Because the relationship with the immediate supervisor, more than anything else, determines the individual's success and potential long-term viability. Relationships with coworkers, teamwork, and the meaningfulness of the work itself round out the broader categories of how the individual worker feels as part of the broader team.

Gossips, snitches, and rumormongers, however, will kill camaraderie and trust faster than just about anything. Intercept rumors immediately since they can take on a life of their own and lower productivity and morale if not stopped at their source. See book 4 (*Leadership Defense*) of *The Paul Falcone Workplace Leadership Series*—in the section titled "Dealing with Gossips, Rumormongers, and Snitches"—for more information on how to effectively handle such challenging behaviors.

PLAN AHEAD

All employees want some sense of job security regarding their future with the company. They likewise want to understand how their efforts contribute to the organization's larger goals, mission, and vision. Share information generously. Ensure that people understand the *why* of your questions so they can tie their recommended solutions to the broader picture. Help them learn about your organization and build upon their knowledge by collecting data in scorecards, dashboards, and other forms of data intelligence gathering. Remember that best-in-class companies are recognized by long-term tenure because of the sheer amount of institutional knowledge that's retained over time. Helping employees plan ahead and understand their role relative to the company's future challenges is a healthy kind of glue that binds people to your company for the long haul.

20

SALVAGING RESTLESS TOP PERFORMERS
APPEALING TO PERSONAL
CAREER DEVELOPMENT NEEDS

P oll after poll reveals that some 50–75 percent of employees say they would leave their current companies once the right opportunity arises, and members of your staff may be no exception. How do you identify subordinates who may be vulnerable to becoming "recruiter's bait," and more important, what can you do now to stimulate their loyalty to your company, so they don't leave when temptation calls?

First, remember that it's not so much employee *satisfaction* that's at issue as much as employee *engagement*. Keeping subordinates engaged in their work, helping them feel like they make a true difference, and helping them build their resumes and skill sets is the stuff of great leadership. In fact, the glue that binds someone to any company at any given time is the learning curve. Help them to better themselves while benefiting your company, and they'll be both satisfied and engaged. When employees feel engaged and like they're firing on all pistons, no amount of money (within reason) will likely be able to entice them away.

But employee disengagement can be insidious and seep into your workplace over time. After all, no job is great enough for the human spirit. Once an "us-versus-them" entitlement mentality takes hold, it can be difficult going back. In such cases, the grass tends to become a lot greener anywhere other than at your company, and by that time, it may be too late to turn things around.

People remain engaged when they receive recognition and appreciation for a job well done. They're satisfied when they experience open communication and trust with their immediate supervisor, and they excel when they believe that they've got longer-term opportunities available to them beyond their current role in the organization. In short, there is a *psychic income* at work that makes people feel socially accepted and respected.

In contrast, disengagement may show itself in several common ways, both subtle and overt, including a sudden nine-to-five mentality, an unwillingness to participate in social events outside of the office, or a tendency to "fox-hole" oneself apart from one's peers. It becomes most noticeable when someone who's normally outgoing and enthusiastic seems to fall by the wayside and has nothing positive to contribute. Sometimes it shows itself quietly with raised eyebrows and sighs of apathy; other times, it results in open challenges to authority or shouting matches with peers. Whether the change is obvious or intuitive, assume that you may be vulnerable to losing your superstar once opportunity comes knocking because work at your office just isn't fun, rewarding, or exciting for that individual anymore.

Reengaging the superstar isn't all that hard to do if you, the manager, have the desire to do so. First, ask your employee what's important to him. The most effective strategies focus on the particular individual's needs. The key issue to ask yourself is, "Is there *trust* in the relationship?" It's one thing to say you *like* your boss, and it's another to say you *respect* your boss. But *trust* is the third and most critical element: If a strong bond of trust exists, then assume you could fix just about anything. If it's missing, however, then you may be best off allowing the employee to self-select out of the company and start looking for a replacement.

Assuming that trust is indeed present in your relationship, the first move will be yours as the supervisor to raise the subject this way:

> Joe, I wanted to meet with you one-on-one to gain a feel for your level of satisfaction in your current role and with our company in general. I'll make no bones about it—I want to keep you, and I want to make sure you're satisfied and feeling engaged about our organization and your role in it. I see you as an integral part of the future of this company and our department. I realize we may not have any promotional opportunities for you right now, and I can't tell you what our year-end merit budgets will look like, but I can tell you that I want to help prepare you for greater responsibilities within the firm, and I'd like to speak with you now about how to do that.

With such a solid verbal commitment (and hopefully an equally solid performance review and individual development plan on file), it's time to get creative. This creativity will be a function of your industry, geography, and company history as well as your subordinate's personal interests, but let's take a look at an example from the discipline of human resources management.

Your director of staffing is doing a stellar job identifying talent and closing offers with difficult-to-find job candidates, but you suspect competitors that know of his reputation may recruit him. Besides, you believe that he may feel that his position is becoming less challenging and more of a "maintenance mode" type of job. Maybe this individual wants to eventually run his own HR department, or maybe he prefers to remain in the sub-discipline of recruitment over the long term. You won't know until you ask, so look for creative alternatives that could motivate this individual to stay with your company for his own good despite an onslaught of job offers that may come his way.

By making individual commitments to your key "keepers," you'll be helping them gain skills, knowledge, and competencies that they may not yet possess. You'll also identify skill gaps and developmental opportunities to motivate them and enhance your own reputation as a true leader and career coach. It's a win-win for all because your proactive outreach will have prevented a top performer from leaving. In addition, you will have saved the company the time and expense of having to recruit and train a replacement, and you will have reengaged someone who, consciously or not, may have simply been cruising along unaware of his own career desires and needs.

Is there a risk that you'll be waking a "sleeping giant" who's now considering making unrealistic salary and promotion demands? After all, Joe wasn't complaining to you outright—you simply suspected that he might be feeling disengaged and under-whelmed by his current level of responsibility. Yes. There's a slight risk that you'll inadvertently raise Joe's expectations and create a morale problem by not offering him more money and a promotion along with these other activities. But if there's trust in the relationship to begin with, this shouldn't be an issue. Besides, if you preempt your conversation by telling him this is about career development and not so much about immediate salary or promotional changes, you'll set expectations correctly so that your praise and recognition of his work doesn't immediately go to his head.

In essence, you'll have initiated a "counteroffer negotiation" before it was ever needed and in a much friendlier light. Challenging your employees to reengage in their roles and reinvest in their careers will no doubt make your own career a lot more rewarding and fun. You may just find that creating new career opportunities for those you care most about in the workplace will take on a new life of its own.

21

"STAY INTERVIEWS" TROUNCE COUNTEROFFERS EVERY TIME

Top performers will always naturally have the most options available to them should they opt to pursue greener pastures at some point. And who could blame them? Many workers feel like they've been treading water career-wise for years but fear changing companies for reasons of job security. How do you get ahead of this natural curve in a top performer's career trajectory and keep your best and brightest motivated and engaged? And how do you obviate the need for a counteroffer discussion once the employee you count on most comes into your office with a letter of resignation?

There's no doubt about it: once an employee submits a letter of resignation, a mental break with your organization has already occurred. And you don't want to be forced into discussions that sound like this:

Oh, I didn't know you were unhappy! Why didn't you tell me you wanted more money or responsibility? Let me know what your new title and salary will look like and give me a few days to see if we could put together a package that will keep you happy.

Just promise me you won't make a decision yet until you hear what we come back with. . . .

Unfortunately, this real-life scenario is playing itself out more and more in organizations across the country. But could it be avoided? Was there something the manager could have done proactively to evade this snare? The answer, of course, is yes: surprises regarding your best performers are avoidable if you're in tune with their career needs and longer-term goals.

So, if you've been taking this for granted and haven't had this type of conversation in a while (or never at all before), now's your opportunity to open up the lines of communication and go through a "resignation drill" to ensure that your best and brightest are fully engaged, excited, and in some sort of learning curve that keeps them motivated and committed to your team and company.

Stay interviews don't only have to focus on your top performers—the top 20 percent of your workers who set the standard for performance and productivity and make your life so much easier. They can just as easily apply to the 70 percent of your workers who populate the middle of the bell curve performance-wise. But starting with your top performers makes inherent sense. Communicating your appreciation of their contributions and demonstrating interest in their future career development within your organization in general and on your team specifically is critical. This type of engagement exercise shouldn't ever seem artificial, superficial, or insincere, but it may be something that your people aren't used to or otherwise expecting from you. Therefore, here's a way to ease into a conversation with someone you'd hate to lose to some other organization should an opportunity come their way.

First, some background context: if a headhunter approached one of your top employees with an enticing opportunity at a competitor firm, the headhunter might ask:

What's your reason for wanting to leave your present company?

What would have to change in your present position for you to consider staying?

What's your next logical move in career progression if you remain with your current employer, and how long would it take you to get there?

How would your top-performing workers respond? A typical response from an unhappy or otherwise disengaged employee might be:

Well, there's really no room for growth at my current company. I don't see myself learning anything new—I'm just doing volumes of the same work that I've been doing for the past few years. And I just feel like I'm treading water career-wise. There's little opportunity here, either in terms of dollars or new responsibilities.

If you suspect that one or more of your key players might respond to a headhunter's call in similar fashion, it's time for you to spend some time with them and get to know more about their current level of job satisfaction and engagement. In other words, use this starting point as an entrée into deeper discussions about their ideas for improving the workflow in your area, building their own career while remaining at your company, and finding new ways of reinventing themselves in light of your department's changing needs.

Start your discussion by asking your staffer how he'd rank his experience at your organization in terms of how happy, engaged, and rewarded he feels. Also, does he feel like he gets to do his very best work every day? If he asks why you're asking, just tell him that you are looking to spice things up a bit in terms of raising the engagement level of the people on your team. But you're starting with your star players first to gauge how they're feeling and how they think the rest of the team might respond to similar questions.

Expect an answer of seven or eight on a scale of ten (ten being extremely happy, one being unbelievably miserable). It's only natural that most employees are discontent to some degree at any given time. Although most won't volunteer that type of feedback directly unless you ask, they typically won't give you, their supervisor, a score lower than seven for fear that you'll think they're unmotivated or otherwise looking to leave. Likewise, anyone who defines themselves as a ten probably is "blowing smoke" rather than being totally honest with you (barring any recent promotions or special events that really benefited them). If the average response, then, will typically come in around an eight, ask the follow-up questions: (a) "Why are you an eight?" and then, (b) "What would make you a ten?"

The goal here is to find out, in a very subtle and sincere way, where they stand relative to your organization and how vulnerable they might be to becoming "recruiter's bait" to a headhunter's call. To drive the conversation even further, ask them what would motivate them relative to the six variables that follow.

"Which of the six following categories hold the most significance for you career-wise at this point?"

Career progression through the ranks and opportunities for promotion and advancement

Lateral assumption of increased job responsibilities and skill building (for example, rotational assignments in other areas, overseas opportunities, and the like)

Acquisition of new technical skills (for example, via external training and certification)

Development of stronger leadership, management, or administrative skills

Work-life balance and flexibility

Money and other forms of compensation

Although almost all will initially comment on the money/compensation invitation—after all, who wouldn't want more money?—most will quickly shift over to one of the other five areas, which are the real drivers in terms of their motivation to remain with or leave your organization. Use this conversational format to launch into more in-depth discussions about each of your key performer's needs, wants, and desires and then ask for suggestions in terms of how to get them there. Yes, you run the risk of opening up pie-in-the-sky wish lists, but in a one-on-one setting, the chances of unleashing a runaway train of unrealistic expectations diminish. Instead, ensure that you understand what's driving your top performers and how vulnerable you and your company might be to losing them.

If your approach is sincere and selfless and comes from the heart, your employees will respect the effort that you're making, and that alone could go a long way in strengthening your working relationship. Of course, you have to be prepared to follow up on requests for promotions, equity adjustments, and the like, but you can always clarify up front that you can't make any promises or necessarily control the budget constraints that the organization is facing. Explain that the purpose of your conversation is not only to gauge how they're feeling about the organization—a mini climate survey of sorts—but to remind them how much you value them and appreciate their contributions. Tell them outright that you wouldn't want to lose them to a random headhunter's call, and this kind of "stay interview" is far more valuable than an exit interview after the fact.

Finally, confirm that you want to encourage them to develop a realistic and customized individual development (aka retention) plan that will help them prepare for their next move in career progression. Likewise, ask for their input now in terms of what can be improved, made more efficient, reinvented, or re-created within your department and how you both can partner as coleaders to make things better for the team in terms of increasing their confidence level and willingness to stretch the rubber band a bit.

Start the conversation now. Make your key performers a critical part of the team's performance turnaround. Listen to what they're saying and look for new ways of helping them build their career internally within your organization—whether vertically, horizontally, or via a renewed learning curve. Engaging your best and brightest before they're lured to greener pastures is a healthy and proactive measure to avoid counteroffers after the mental break has been made. Stay interviews and resignation drills are a practical and smart approach to raising both key employee engagement and retention.

22

IF YOU'RE GOING TO MAKE A COUNTEROFFER, MAKE SURE YOU DO IT RIGHT

Stay interviews represent the proactive side of keeping your employees engaged and tuned in so they find no need to look for greener pastures elsewhere; in contrast, counteroffer discussions—while sometimes necessary—are more reactive and dramatic in nature. In general, counteroffers should always remain the exception, not the rule. The primary reason is because once employees go through the mental separation process of terminating their employment, an attitudinal break typically occurs that can't easily be undone. In addition, appearing to throw dollars at people to stay aboard once they've committed themselves to another employer could be perceived as a desperate move on the company's part and poor career management on the individual's part. Ask headhunters if counteroffers work, and they'll quickly tell you that in a majority of cases, employees who accept counteroffers will likely be gone within six months anyway because the underlying reasons for their dissatisfaction don't often change.

Therefore, barring sincere management intervention, the additional cash from a counteroffer may simply delay the inevitable, and employees who accept counteroffers for fear of change or out of a sense of guilt eventually come to realize that if the original reasons they were considering leaving haven't changed, then leaving still makes sense. Add that to the fact that companies that engage in counteroffers on a regular and consistent basis run the risk of creating a moral hazard with the organization. Coworkers watch the pattern play itself out time and again and come to reason, "This company is cheap and won't do anything for you to keep you happy, so you have to give notice to get noticed and leverage more money." Not a good strategy at all, and this can, in fact, serve as a trap for employers who throw money at workers this late in the game to convince them to stay.

That being said, there may be times when a counteroffer makes sense in terms of dealing with an employee's resignation. The key lies in knowing how to structure the counteroffer to help the individual reconnect with the organization and regain a sense of value—both in terms of his impact on the organization and his ability to build his career there. But that may be more easily said than done because it takes honesty and transparency on both sides to make the outcome successful. Both sides—the company and the worker—must readily admit their shortcomings in allowing the situation to have digressed to this crisis stage, and both must be willing to make a sincere and conscious effort to turn things around. With a double commitment from both secured, the healing process can begin, and the individual can go about reinventing his relationship with the organization from a fresh perspective.

Here are two simple guidelines to follow if you, the employer, are sincerely thinking that a counteroffer would be effective in dire circumstances where an employee has tendered his resignation. First, if you are deeply committed to listening, hearing what this individual's issues are, and partnering to turn around the true core problems that caused the individual to look to leave in the first place, there's a chance that an honest employer intervention in the form of a counteroffer could work. But it must be sincere, selfless, and focused on the individual's needs. Throwing money or a title at the problem and then forgetting that it ever occurred is a formula for disaster because it simply delays the inevitable. And that's not fair to your employee who may be walking away from a great opportunity elsewhere.

Second, prepare for the exercise as if you had no money or title changes available to offer. Would you still be able to make a compelling argument as to why this individual might want to remain with your company? What else—beyond money and title—could change, and what would that renewed relationship look like? True, you arguably wouldn't extend a counteroffer without trying to meet the demands of the new opportunity that's been offered, but if you're not looking at this holistically and in a broader sense than simply in terms of dollars and titles, you may be missing the point of the whole intervention. In short, if you're not willing to engage and invest in a "hypercare" opportunity in which you'll dedicate yourself to this individual for the next three to six months to ensure that everything remains on track in terms of the agreements you're making now, then forego the counteroffer and wish him well in his new job. We're talking true engagement that's required here, and that includes ongoing partnering and follow-up.

A genuine counteroffer discussion might include the fact that there have been few internal opportunities to promote or scarce bonus rounds because of the economy. Despite those limitations, you want your employee to recognize that you see her as a "keeper" and you're willing to build a longer-term individual development plan around her career desires. First, you'll obviously want to listen to what brought her to the decision to leave your organization, and you'll respectfully inquire as to the terms of her new opportunity. Second, you'll have to share up front that you can't make any promises without getting senior leadership and budget approval. But with her help, you can learn what might make her want to consider staying. Finally, you can offer opportunities that she might not have thought of, including trips to the corporate home office, a new educational program that might result in certification or licensure, an opportunity to learn another part of the business, a better work-life balance, or something similar.

Whatever she decides at that point, you have to respect her decision. If she opts to stay, don't celebrate too quickly: realize the hard work is just about to begin, as you'll have lots to do to deliver on the promises made. If she opts to leave, make it safe for her to do so: engage her services in finding her replacement, and consider throwing a small farewell party so others can celebrate her contributions over the years. There's no reason to end on a sour note: in fact, if she's moving into a higher role with more responsibility at the new firm, you and your team can celebrate her achievement, which she likely would not have been able to accomplish without the work she did for your organization. "Healthy turnover" is all about professional and career development. Yes, it hurts when a top performer leaves, but it gives new opportunities to other players on the team who will likely step up to seize the coveted spot being left behind.

With such a respectful, selfless, and well-thought-out counteroffer strategy lined up, you'll no doubt have a chance at retaining this individual. Even if you're not successful, you can at least rest assured that word will get out that you handled the whole matter professionally, that you put the individual's career interests above your own needs, and that you were very "cool and classy" about the whole thing. The outcome may be beyond your control; however, the strategy you employ will make you feel good personally and distinguish you as a true leader within your company.

23

RECOGNIZING BURNOUT AND REENGAGING YOUR EMPLOYEES BASED ON THEIR INDIVIDUAL NEEDS

Workplace burnout is a state of emotional or physical exhaustion that is brought on by long periods of stress and frustration. It's an all-too-common result of ongoing pressure, stress, and fear about job security, performance demands, company health, and the like. With manic job markets with massive upticks followed by significant downturns, workers at all levels feel the pressure inherent in managing a career in corporate America. Perhaps you feel the emotional drain as well from constantly trying to keep your employees engaged and happy. Whatever the case and however you and your employees got here, the results aren't pretty: shorter tempers, snippy and condescending responses, excessively long evening and weekend working hours, loss of work-life integration, and other classic signs of disengagement may be at hand.

Whenever you sense that one of your team members may be suffering from career burnout or work overload, start first by recognizing where those feelings are coming from. If working long days with no breaks is the challenge, then scheduling time away from the office may be a simple and effective remedy. Yes, that means that work will likely pile up pending the individual's return, but maybe you could help with that temporarily by assigning new incoming work to other staff members on a rotational basis. Do this for all your employees and give them all a much-needed break from the action.

If everyone's eating lunch at their desks on a regular basis, then it may be time to put your foot down: start slowly by assigning one day per week where you all get out of the office to eat together. Likewise, make it a priority to go for a group walk around your building or through your neighborhood. A twenty-minute walk at 3:00 p.m. is healthy for everyone—including yourself—and gives you a chance to bond with one another and breathe some fresh air. You could even consider it a form of teambuilding if you can come up with an exercise to engage in while you're walking.

Likewise, remember that even a small change can make a big difference. For starters, limit the number of emails that you're all sending one another. Email inboxes are filled to the brim these days, but little emails that say "Thank you" and "Much appreciated" can be knocked off the list with one simple instruction to your team, thereby thinning the herd of those little critters in your inbox. Likewise, make it a rule to limit email length to only that which you can see without scrolling down your smartphone screen with your thumb (that is, about two to three sentences). For anything longer than that, simply add a final sentence that reads, "If you'd like more background, please see below." But at least you'll train your people to provide you with snapshots of data so that you can get the main message without reading through a five-paragraph missive that leaves you to tease out the key points.

Since we're talking about email challenges that lead to employee burnout, instruct your staffers to use the subject line more effectively. A subject line that reads "FYI" doesn't help much because you have no operational context to prioritize. On the other hand, if the subject line reads "Change in California paid sick leave calculation (ninety-day look-back required)," you'll have a much clearer understanding of the resolution required before you even read the message.

Besides massive email volume contributing to employee burnout, the second largest frustration factor typically has to do with the number of meetings that workers must attend during the day. If everyone's in meetings six or seven hours a day, then those emails can't be addressed until after hours or on weekends. Therefore, scour your meeting lists, write them down to see which ones can be combined or eliminated, and challenge all but the most critical. Too many meetings simply cause information overload, and it's not true that everyone needs to know everything all the time. FYIs are helpful, but not if they take people out of circulation to the detriment of the work they're doing.

Remember as well that burnout may be the result of being overworked or underappreciated, bored, or otherwise depressed. It's easy to feel understimulated in a work environment where career progression has been stymied at most organizations due to the ongoing downsizing exercises that continue to mark the landscape in corporate America. Vertical career progression isn't necessarily a thing of the past, but there are relatively fewer opportunities to promote now than there have been historically due to ongoing changes from technology and globalization. In cases in which you suspect that people may feel depressed about the daily nature of their work or their inability to get ahead, fear not: a simple solution may lie in limited rotational assignments or job-shadowing exercises in which employees can spend an hour, a day, or a week working side by side with other members of the team to learn about new roles and focus areas. Maybe you can "lend out" a staffer to help another team with a particular project, with other members of your team covering for the individual during the temporary period of absence.

In short, if your employees dread coming to work on Monday mornings or are otherwise crabby with one another and short with you, then you've got to step in and find out what the key drivers of their dissatisfaction are. And you'll only learn if you ask. Ask all team members individually where they stand on a scale of one to ten in terms of feeling overworked or undervalued. Ask what they would like to see the team doing differently or what they would focus on if they could change one thing about how the work gets done in your office. Instruct the staff to develop three takeaways that are designed to lessen their workload, relieve their stress, or add exercise and breaks to their day. And don't forget about the benefits of a hybrid remote work structure: permitting employees to work from home one or two days per week can go a long way on cutting down commuter stress while allowing employees the flexibility and independence to get things done their way and on their own terms. There are many opportunities if you allow room for them. You'll only know if you ask for input.

There are solutions when group dynamics take a turn for the worse. Lack of enthusiasm, isolation, decreases in productivity, and overall apathy or apparent frustration won't lend themselves to a quick-fix solution. In most cases, real and significant changes will need to be discussed, evaluated, and implemented. But this is your shop, and as the leader, you have enormous influence in these areas to make things happen. You have it within your power to reshape people's work lives, to turn around lackluster performers who may be feeling burned out by the workload, understimulated by treading water career-wise, or otherwise un-derappreciated for what they contribute. As with most things in life, however, your experience is created internally. Change your perspective and you'll change your perception: you can change your mind any time about how something affects you. Use this opportunity to turn around your team, focus on opportunities that are important to them, and move everyone forward in a healthy and renewed spirit.

PUTTING YOUR EMPLOYEES FIRST

EVEN ABOVE YOUR CUSTOMERS AND SHAREHOLDERS

Organizational reward systems—employee of the month, anniversary awards, "applause" bulletin boards, "Wall of Fame" photos, and on-the-spot special recognition awards—are great. But this section's focus goes beyond those activities and programs to speak about increasing awareness and sensitivity to a soft skill that's arguably one of the most critical drivers of business success: empathy. It's about recognizing that the most effective type of recognition occurs at the individual level. It assumes that providing recognition is not an optional activity but an integral part of your organizational strategy.

A motivational work environment rests on:

- developing open and honest relationships through communication;
- building a positive team and family spirit via trust; and
- sustaining a continued focus on career growth and development.

As such, it recognizes that the single most important variable in employee performance and productivity is the quality of the relationship between employees and their supervisors. Further, workplace wisdom suggests that, besides supporting their families, work allows employees an opportunity to make a difference. They want to understand how they fit with the company's vision and how they can contribute.

Therefore, on a more practical basis, placing your focus on employee engagement over customer satisfaction will likely yield happier, more loyal customers. That's why organizations often create mission statements that reverse the traditional order of placing employees at the bottom of the pecking order (that is, behind customers, products, and shareholders). What companies are realizing is that their most important assets literally walk out the door every night. Simply stated, when it comes to generating excellent customer service strategies, the tide is shifting away from putting the focus on the customer to placing it on the employee who delivers the customer experience.

Vineet Nayar, CEO of HCL Technologies and author of *Employees First, Customers Second: Turning Conventional Management Upside Down,* said simply that your employees are the gateway to customer satisfaction, and if they aren't happy, the customer isn't going to be happy. Richard Branson, CEO of Virgin, famously stated: "The formula is quite simple: happy employees equal happy customers. Similarly, an unhappy employee can ruin the brand experience for not just one, but numerous customers." And Southwest Airlines consistently emphasizes this philosophy behind its employee-centric approach to doing business and creating long-term value.

Gallup has been measuring employee engagement for years and found conclusive evidence in their research that the level of engaged employees a company has is directly proportional to its profitability levels. Implementing an employee-first culture builds trust, holds people accountable, and rewards companies financially because of their ability to attract and retain the best and brightest. Besides, they're more fun and creative. If customers are the lifeblood of your company, then your workers are the veins. Showing that you care for them—even more than you value your customers—sends a message regarding your priorities and their well-being. At that point, you can unleash all those happy employees to be more productive because they want to be . . . not because they have to be.

▪ ▪ ▪

Leadership is a privilege. As a leader, you've been given the ability to change lives. It's your responsibility to coach people to be the best they can be. In fact, leadership is the greatest gift the workplace has to offer because of its exponential return on investment: you grow teams, you become someone's favorite boss, you model servant leadership, and you pay the gift of enlightened leadership forward. In exchange for your efforts, others learn to grow teams, become more engaged in their own careers, develop a heightened sense of self-awareness and career introspection, and serve as role models to others. Leadership offense strategies help you build team muscle. You now have the opportunity to capitalize on people's strengths, challenge your superstars, move the middle 70 percent to higher levels of performance, and develop an achievement mentality in all you're privileged to serve.

It's time to unleash your leadership potential to transform the careers and lives of your staff members to higher states of meaning, purpose, and contribution. And with this simple change in your fundamental thought about who you are and who you choose to be, you are in turn gifted with increased self-awareness and transformational change. What you want for yourself, give to another. What comes from you returns to you. And so, the circle is complete. Thank you for allowing me to partner with you down this path and coach you on the power you hold to positively influence those around you. Remember, the greatest leaders aren't judged by the number of followers they have; they're evaluated on the greatest number of leaders they in turn create. Now is your opportunity to create great leaders, workplaces, and companies. It's in many ways simpler than you think and easier than we tend to make it. Great leadership is yours for the asking, and there's no better way of achieving it than by giving it away. After all, you can't give away something that you don't already possess. Share your leadership wisdom abundantly and make of your life a gift.

INDEX

ABOUT THE AUTHOR

Paul Falcone (www.PaulFalconeHR.com) is the chief human resources officer (CHRO) of the Motion Picture and Television Fund in Woodland Hills, California, where he's responsible for all aspects of HR leadership and strategy. He's the former CHRO of the Nickelodeon Animation Studios and head of international human resources for Paramount Pictures in Hollywood. Paul served as head of HR for the TV production unit of NBCUniversal, where he oversaw HR operations for NBC's late night and primetime programming lineup, including *The Tonight Show*, *Saturday Night Live*, and *The Office*. Paul is a renowned expert on effective interviewing and hiring, performance management, and leadership development, especially in terms of helping companies build higher-performing leadership teams. He also has extensive experience in healthcare/biotech and financial services across international, nonprofit, and union environments.

Paul is the author of a number of HarperCollins Leadership, AMACOM, and SHRM books, many of which have been ranked on Amazon as #1 bestsellers in the areas of human resources management, labor and employment law, business mentoring and coaching, communication in management, and business decision-making and problem-solving. Bestselling books like *101 Tough Conversations to Have with Employees*, *101 Sample Write-Ups for Documenting Employee Performance*

Problems, and *96 Great Interview Questions to Ask Before You Hire* have been translated into Chinese, Vietnamese, Korean, Indonesian, and Turkish.

Paul is a certified executive coach through the Marshall Goldsmith Stakeholder Centered Coaching program, a long-term contributor to SHRM.org and *HR Magazine*, and an adjunct faculty member in UCLA Extension's School of Business and Management, where he's taught courses on workplace ethics, recruitment and selection, legal aspects of human resources management, and international human resources. He is an accomplished keynote presenter, inhouse trainer, and webinar facilitator in the areas of talent management and effective leadership communication.